Literature Review and Research Design

Designing a research project is possibly the most difficult task a dissertation writer faces. It is fraught with uncertainty: what is the best subject? What is the best method? For every answer found, there are often multiple subsequent questions, so it's easy to get lost in theoretical debates and buried under a mountain of literature.

This book looks at literature review in the process of research design, and how to develop a research practice that will build skills in reading and writing about research literature—skills that remain valuable in both academic and professional careers. Literature review is approached as a process of engaging with the discourse of scholarly communities that will help graduate researchers refine, define, and express their own scholarly vision and voice. This orientation on research as an exploratory practice, rather than merely a series of predetermined steps in a systematic method, allows the researcher to deal with the uncertainties and changes that come with learning new ideas and new perspectives.

The focus on the practical elements of research design makes this book an invaluable resource for graduate students writing dissertations. Practicing research allows room for experiment, error, and learning, ultimately helping graduate researchers use the literature effectively to build a solid scholarly foundation for their dissertation research project.

Dave Harris is a writing coach who helps authors develop productive writing practices, using principles from design methods, philosophy of science, and cognitive science. With Jean-Pierre Protzen, he is author of *The Universe of Design* (2010, Routledge) and, alone, author of *Getting the Best of Your Dissertation* (2015, Thought Clearing). Find him on the web at www.thoughtclearing.com

"Unlike other books on research, this book does not prescribe methods or recipes. Rather, it feels like one is sitting with an experienced dissertation coach, having a series of short conversations about the tacit knowledge that underlies the various aspects of research practice. After reading this book, novice researchers will have a better understanding of how the literature supports and brings out a researcher's own voice."

Arnold Wentzel, author of Creative Research in Economics *(Routledge, 2016) and* A Guide to Argumentative Research Writing and Thinking *(Routledge, 2017)*

Literature Review and Research Design

A Guide to Effective Research Practice

Dave Harris

Routledge
Taylor & Francis Group

LONDON AND NEW YORK

First published 2020
by Routledge
2 Park Square, Milton Park, Abingdon, Oxon OX14 4RN

and by Routledge
52 Vanderbilt Avenue, New York, NY 10017

Routledge is an imprint of the Taylor & Francis Group, an informa business

British Library Cataloguing-in-Publication Data
A catalogue record for this book is available from the British Library

Library of Congress Cataloging-in-Publication Data
A catalog record has been requested for this book

ISBN: 978-0-367-25036-2 (hbk)
ISBN: 978-0-367-25037-9 (pbk)
ISBN: 978-0-429-28566-0 (ebk)

Typeset in Galliard
by Swales & Willis, Exeter, Devon, UK

Contents

Introduction   viii
Acknowledgements   xiii

Part I
On research   1

1   Research philosophy   3

A story about the world—your own version   4
Fact, not fiction   7
Uncertainty   9
The community of researchers   11
The research literature: a conversation among scholars   13
Project 1: what does research do for you?   15

2   Research practice   18

Your vision, your purposes   19
Allocation of resources   22
Research design   24
Defining the research question is a significant problem   26
The problem of learning   27
Use what you already know   29
Writing and thinking   31
Practice: writing is a skill to develop   32
Rhetoric and persuading your community   34
Cultivating confidence   36
Finishing your projects   37
Project 2: the practice of research   38

Part II
Reading literature   41

3   Attitude   45

Reasons to read scholarly literature for research design   46
Reasons to read 2: personal purpose   48
How to read: your attitude   49
Heroes and villains   52
Why is so much academic writing bad?   55
Different definitions, different ideas   58
Breaking down arguments   60
Finding the sources for your own ideas   61
Project 3: being critical   64

4   Managing the literature   68

Managing an entire discourse   68
Reviewing the literature   70
Record keeping   72
Using what you have read   74
Finding and selecting literature   75
Accept practical limits   78
Seek efficiency: issues in selecting literature   80
Iterative reading: from quick reviews toward deep reading   82
First iteration: title and publication information   84
Second iteration: abstract   86
Third iteration: single sections   89
Project 4: managing the literature   90

5   Deep reading   94

Direct models   95
Motivation   97
Audience   98
Use of other literature   100
Style and rhetorical models   102
Questions: from concept to practical research   104
Reading checklist/questionnaire   106
Project 5: deep reading   108

Part III
Writing about literature

111

6   Writing with literature   **115**

Write with purpose   116
Drafts and feedback   119
Target lengths   121
Focal, contextual, and tangential materials   122
Situating your work   124
In conversation with heroes and villains   127
Audience   130
Focus on your own work   133
Paraphrasing   134
Project 6: writing with literature   136

7   Writing a literature review   **137**

What is a literature review?   138
The purpose of a research background literature review   140
Writing about search terms   143
Voice   145
How short can a literature review be?   146
Start from the core, and work outward   147
Writing a literature review—structural concerns   149
Project 7: writing a skeleton literature review   153

Conclusion   156
Suggested readings   158
Index   160

Introduction

There is an old joke that a tourist in New York City, seeking directions, asks a musician, "How do you get to Carnegie Hall?" The musician replies "practice." For this book, that could be a model: practice is the answer. How do you perform a literature review? Practice. How do you design a research project? Practice. How do you finish your independent design project (especially your dissertation or thesis)? Practice.

Research is a process that is commonly associated with methods and systematic procedures. The notion is that the researcher following a method will produce good research. If you follow a systematic method to do a literature review, for example, you'll do a successful literature review. Unfortunately, it's not that simple. While there is a crucial role for methods in research, designing a research project involves many dimensions that no method can encompass.

The design of a research project is a problem of crucial import for researchers, especially graduate students carrying out their first independent project, which is often the dissertation or thesis. Most graduate students have excelled in their academic work throughout their lives. And yet, when it's time for the independent research project—the dissertation—many of these excellent students get stuck. Dissertations are so notoriously difficult that the informal "degree" of ABD (All But Dissertation) is familiar throughout academia due to the very large proportion of students who excelled in everything but didn't finish their dissertation.

Though I lack empirical data, I would argue that a large number of these excellent students struggle in the process of research design—the process of choosing a topic and moving from that topic to a plan for a research project using appropriate research methods. And one large trap in the process can be a literature review. The same conscientious students who excelled in coursework can get stuck, saying, "I just need to read a few more articles before I start." Or they can write extremely long literature reviews and say, "well, I still need to add another section." More than a few, I think, simply get overwhelmed by it all and become paralyzed. If you are seeking a doctorate, you are expected to be something of an expert on your subject, are you not? But what is a reasonable standard? How much literature review is enough?

This book is about using literature effectively in the process of designing, developing, and completing a research project. It is aimed at graduate students who will be required to write a dissertation or thesis, and who may have little previous experience with the practicalities of that process.

Practice and method

If there are parts of research that cannot be guided by method, as I claim above, what are those spots, and how does the researcher negotiate them?

The places where method cannot help are innumerable. The most consequential decisions you have to make are not guided by any method. Your choice of topic, for example, cannot be made by any method. There might be some systematic techniques to suggest a topic, but you don't have to do what a system says, do you? For that matter, what method do you use to choose a method? And, in addition to the purely theoretical and intellectual issues that influence the design of a research project, there are all sorts of personal and practical dimensions that influence your choices. Your choice of topic or method, for starters, will influence which professors you work with.

How does the researcher negotiate these concerns where method cannot help? Practice. Of course, it has to be the right practice, with the right intentions and purposes. That, in a nutshell, is what this book hopes to explain: why and how you can develop your own research practice that will help you design, develop, and execute your own independent research project.

Practice is a process of growth, exploration, and experimentation—all of which are fundamental to research as well. By experimenting, the practitioner (researcher) develops skill and judgment.

The literature review trap

Academic literature is complicated, dense, often poorly written, and there's a lot of it. If you're beginning work on your own independent research project, you probably face expectations that you will do some sort of literature review as part of your dissertation work. While the literature is an invaluable resource—use it to build a foundation for your own research!—with the wrong approach it can become a quagmire into which you sink, thinking "If I just read the right book, I'll be saved!"

Part of the problem is the idea of "literature review"—it is a phrase whose meaning is not fully determined. "Literature review" can refer to a process of reading scholarly literature or to a piece of writing about scholarly literature. It can refer to the quick, informal activities of a few hours, or a highly formalized research study. There are different kinds of literature reviews that suit different purposes, and if you do the wrong kind, you can expend a lot of effort without making progress.

This book is less interested in "literature review," per se, than in using academic literature in the process of research design. How do you read to find sources of guidance? How do you write about it to get support for your work from your research community (starting with your professors)? And yes, a partial answer to both those questions is: practice!

As a researcher, and especially as a graduate student trying to write a dissertation or thesis, the truly difficult task is to design and develop a research project and to bring that project to completion. Getting caught up in doing a "literature review" takes time away from the more important question of research design.

Your research project, your vision, your voice

This book grew out of my work helping dissertation writers and my sense that many got stuck not for lack of ability, but rather because of an idealized understanding of research and poor sense of their own place in the research community. In particular, this plays out in how people approach the literature: too many read like students doing coursework, rather than as scholars who have something to add to the scholarly discourse. Dissertations and theses are for original research, and the way to do that is to develop your own vision, your own voice, and your own research project to add to the scholarly discourse in your field.

This book, then, is about how you develop a research practice that leads to development of your own voice and your own research project, and how you use the literature to support that practice.

If I could give you a road map to designing the perfect research project or to executing the perfect literature review, I would. But each individual researcher has to blaze a new trail—that's part of doing original research.

Instead, I hope to help you develop a practice in which you identify your own purposes and the steps that you can take to complete your project in a reasonable time, with reasonable effort, and, with a little luck, have the whole thing be a positive experience rather than some ordeal through which you suffer to prove your worth.

Book overview

The book begins with a general discussion of research, the basic context in which research literature is created and used, and the purposes for which research literature is developed. This sets up the more specific discussions of how to use research literature in developing your own research.

There are both philosophical and practical limits to research. A practice-based approach to research focuses on generating a reasonable research project, using research literature in that process, and on how to work through spots of uncertainty. Crucially, this book examines the role of community in research and suggests viewing the academic literature as a conversation among scholars.

The second part, on reading, discusses the process of gathering ideas from literature. Of greatest importance, perhaps, is the discussion of the attitude and approach of the independent researcher toward published literature. When you're a student, scholarly literature is typically something you're expected to repeat and explain to your teachers, but when you're a scholar developing your own research, you need to challenge the literature and see what challenges it presents to your research, not just learn it.

The final part of the book focuses on the use of literature in developing your own written work. It is broken in two parts: the first focuses on general issues in writing about literature, and the second focuses on the question of "literature review" and on one particular kind of literature review common in dissertations.

Exercises and projects

Throughout the book is the idea that active practice is the key to success. One of the crucial dimensions of thinking of research as a practice is that one goal of a practice is to develop skills. If you want to know how to have success as a researcher, part of the answer is to practice!

This book is filled with suggestions about developing a practice. It also includes suggested writing activities. With any of these suggestions, feel free to alter them to suit your own purposes. It's less important to do what I suggest than to do something! There is no substitute for practice.

This book offers both quick exercises for exploration and imagination and more extended projects taking more effort to complete. Explore ideas. Experiment with writing and different ways of expressing yourself in writing.

Exercises

Each chapter section ends with some quick exercises. They are often open-ended, and meant as an opportunity to imagine different possibilities. Writing them out will practice your imagination and stretch your ideas (hopefully), and will help improve your skill and ability as a writer. Write quickly and easily, without worrying about what anyone else would think. There are suggested time limits to emphasize engaging quickly. Don't worry about making mistakes (though do try to learn from them). The more you practice writing without worrying about getting it right, the easier it is to write it right when it's time to share something with others.

Projects

Each chapter offers a "project," a larger exercise laid out in greater detail asking for greater engagement. Unlike the exercises, there are no suggested time limits. But, since the time it takes to complete a task is a crucial element in success, it's worth practicing making a schedule and keeping within its time constraints. Set your own time limits for the projects and try to keep to them.

Some of the projects ask you to describe aspects of your own research project. If you have not yet begun to define and design your own dissertation or thesis project, why not start now? Experiment. Make up a possible research project, then go through the chapter's project and see what you learn.

This book is meant to be read fast! (Ok, "quickly")

Follow the main thread. Follow the big ideas. Details are provided to help flesh out and explain the big points, but the big points are what matter.

Acknowledgements

Over the years, I have learned a tremendous amount from the writers with whom I have worked, for which I am grateful and would like to express appreciation. This book is very much a product of what they have taught me.

This book is also a product of what I learned from my graduate school advisor, Jean-Pierre Protzen. As the years pass, my understanding and appreciation of all he gave me grow.

Similarly, thanks to Eve Sweetser and Greig Crysler, without whom I would never have finished my dissertation. Working with dissertation writers, I have frequent reminders of how lucky I was with my committee.

Thanks to Natalya Androsova and Julia Figliotti Riley, who read and gave me feedback on drafts of this book.

Thanks to Brian Francis, Marcia Gorrie, Alan Harris, Suzanne Savell, and Nichole Thomas for general support.

Thanks to Hannah Shakespeare and Routledge for taking on this book.

On research

PART

The general answer to questions about how to do a research project or a literature review may be "practice," but that doesn't give much guidance about how to practice or what to practice. For that, we need to take a look at the general processes of research, your (the researcher's) place in that process, and the role of research literature in that process.

To design a research project effectively, it helps to understand research and the researcher's place—your place—in the world of research. The better you understand how research works, the better you can work to find a research project that will work for you. Complicating the issue, however, are two factors: 1) the more closely you examine the issues of research, the less certain it becomes, and 2) there is a gap between theory and practice.

What are the issues of research? I think that pretty much any scholar trying to explain research to a child, for example, would explain it as the attempt to distinguish fact from fiction or truth from falsity. There is a nice certainty and simplicity to that. Unfortunately, research is rarely certain or simple.

Chapter 1 is concerned with the theoretical issues of research and where the researcher fits in: what is research trying to accomplish? If research is, speaking loosely, the attempt to separate fact from fiction, what are the theoretical concerns of that attempt?

The theoretical issues that shape research are important, but research is not just a theoretical exercise. It is an actual practical activity. It's something on which researchers have to spend time and effort. There is no research that doesn't involve practical activities. Designing a research project may be all prospective, in the sense that you might create a plan for later execution, but it, too, is an activity. The more practical dimensions are the concern of Chapter 2.

Research philosophy

Aiming at the wrong target is never a good way to achieve success. If you have to design a research project, it's important to have reasonable expectations. Idealized views of the scholar may focus on the individual working alone, in the ivory tower, separate from the world, following strict methods, and discovering objective facts that "speak for themselves," as the expression goes. But this perspective is unrealistic. Methods don't have all the answers, facts don't speak for themselves, and scholars work in communities.

Research is about describing and explaining the real world: what is it and how does it work? It wants to tell a coherent story about the world, but not just any story; one that is, in basic terms, fact, not fiction. But separating fact from fiction is not trivial … if, indeed, it is at all possible: there is good reason to believe that uncertainty cannot be eliminated, for all the best efforts of researchers.

Nonetheless, research continues because people have questions and want answers. Although logical certainty may not be available, communities of researchers develop that share ideas that structure their work. Speaking broadly, we can say that all academic researchers share a community and language—one in which a "dissertation" is a major research project done by a student, for example. And then each school is its own community. And each department within a school is a community. And all scholars studying a similar subject form a community, and so on. And the participants in these communities try to talk with each other, about what they have found as well as about the strengths and weaknesses they see in other people's works. This conversation among community members manifests in the research literature.

If you are trying to design a research project for your dissertation, then, the literature can be a guide to how to develop research that will satisfy the expectations and interests of your research community (or communities).

A story about the world—your own version

Researchers do research to tell better stories. Research wants to explain the world, and so it tells stories about how the world works and stories about how research works. A research project will develop when a researcher is trying to tell a story and comes up against a question that wants an answer.

The basic purpose of research is to tell a story about the world. The story must meet academic standards, but it is a story all the same.

Sometimes this is obvious. History is obviously a story—the story of what happened at some past time and place. But the "story" in many fields is not as obvious.

Physics, for example, with its experiments and equations, is not obviously a story. But physics tells the story of how physical objects act or interact. Newton's first law, which states that an object at rest will remain at rest unless acted on by some force, is fundamentally a narrative about the behavior of objects: first there is an object at rest, and as time passes, that object remains at rest, and then, maybe, some force acts on the object and the object responds/reacts in some way.

Present-day scientific explanations—for example, a heliocentric solar system governed by gravity, or the Big Bang—may not appear to be stories, but they replace explanations taken from myth and rely on the same basic narrative structure. A god driving a chariot across the sky is much more obviously a story than saying "the earth rotates on its axis, causing the sun's apparent motion," but both describe a series of events that explain the sun's daily progress across the sky. Explaining the world's creation as the will of a god is an alternative to the Big Bang—both are stories.

Biological sciences tell stories about the behaviors and development of living beings. Chemistry tells of the behaviors of molecules and substances.

Philosophy tells stories of how ideas interact. Descartes's famed "I think, therefore I am" is a narrative of causal behavior, in this case between premises: my thinking implies my existence. Mathematical and logical proofs have similar causal structure: because premise A is true, then premise B must be true, etc.

Psychology tells stories of how the human mind operates. A medical view of psychology might tell the story that some psychological pathology arose through an imbalance of neurotransmitters. A Freudian view might explain that the pathology arose from a childhood event.

Literary Critical Theory tells many different kinds of stories—of how works were created, of how authors thought, of how texts can teach lessons. Reader-response criticism is a story about how a reader interacts with the work. Biographical criticism is a story about how an author's biography shaped a work, or about how a work reveals an author's biography. Psycho-analytic/Freudian criticism tells how an author's writing, like a dream or a slip of the tongue, reveals the author's unconscious.

I emphasize this story-like nature of research because research requires more than just gathering data and then presenting those data to an audience. Research requires trying to weave those data into a larger coherent story that is theoretically or practically significant. Your role is to develop your own version of the larger story, to check that story (or some aspect of it) through a research project, and then to share that with your research community.

In order to explain your work to your community, you want to weave your own story into the stories of other scholars in your community in a way that corrects, complements, or supplements the stories being told by those researchers. Of course, if you have learned anything from your research community—if you have been influenced by your professors or your readings (which is surely to be hoped!)—then the story you want to tell will be shaped by some of the same ideas used by other members of your community.

To find a research question, researchers look for the proverbial "gap in the literature," which is either, 1) something that has not previously been described or explained, or 2) something that has been poorly described or explained. In both cases, such gaps only become visible within the context of a larger coherent story that you are trying to understand and develop.

If your job as an independent researcher is to tell your own story, it prioritizes developing your own ideas over simply learning the stories of others. This means trying to explicate your own story and then reading the research literature (i.e., listening to the scholarly conversation) to see whose stories make sense to you, and how those stories relate to your own. Which voices express ideas that you use in your own stories? Which voices express ideas that you want to explicitly reject? Which can you simply ignore?

If you're studying education, for example, do you agree with all the different pedagogical theories you have read, or do you think that some are better than others? If you're studying literature, do you agree with all the analyses of a given text, and if not, why not? If you're studying biology, do you see any theories of biological processes that you question or places where current biological theory does not have answers?

It would be great to be able to identify a "best" story (or theory) with confidence, but disparate theories can be readily found, each with strengths and weaknesses. The explanation offered by one scholar contradicts that offered by another. While the competition may be good in some ways, it doesn't offer certainty. To tell a coherent story, you must make choices between competing ideas expressed in the literature.

Focus on your idea of how the world works. Identify the questions you have within that story. It is there that research design begins, with a sense of your own story and with a sense of your own questions about that story.

In my experience, one pitfall for many graduate students is looking in the literature to find a theory to use without first thinking about the theories they are currently using. It may be hard to think of your own ideas as being "theories" on a par with ideas in the published literature, but it's with your own ideas that you need to start. If you doubt your own ideas, remember that if you have learned from your professors and your readings, then your ideas have been shaped by other members of your community, so they're not just wild-eyed speculation.

You have to trust what you do know and what makes sense to you, and build from there. What you know may be frustratingly limited, and you may have doubts—that is a condition of scholarship.[1] Despite limits and questions, it's important to make explicit your own coherent story about the world, so that you can decide which questions are crucial to *your* story. You want to be able to learn, not by just absorbing the ideas of others but by developing, refining, revising, and making explicit your own story, and by comparing it to what you read in the literature. Then you can see where there are problems with your own story, allowing you[2] a better opportunity to see how a given theory might address your questions, conflict with your own ideas, or simply be irrelevant (or only tangentially relevant) to your concerns.

In addition to showing the limits of your own understanding, making your own story explicit can often reveal strong scholarly foundations that you did not consciously recognize. I have known more than one scholar who has said, "I need a theoretical framework" and has gone off to read theory, taking for granted the very theories that they already knew and used.

Many scholars doing their first independent research get caught up looking at the stories that others are telling without having a good sense of their own purpose and beliefs, and they get lost following first one theory, then another. The "literature review trap" is, on a certain level, to look for stories in the literature instead of looking for your own. Original research develops from following your own instincts (while also taking guidance from other research).

What is your story? What is the situation in the world that interests you? What are the important and interesting factors in this situation? How do they behave? And how does your story relate to, grow from, compare to, and add to the stories told by other researchers in your field?

When reading scholarly literature, test the authors' ideas against your own: do they make sense in the context of your own story of the world? Or do they make you want to revise your own story in any way to accommodate the new ideas? Or do you simply reject them?

Exercises (30 to 60 seconds each, repeat for 5 to 30 minutes)

What stories do you want to tell or learn more about?

What stories do you want to tell or learn more about in your department, but outside your area of specialization?

What stories do you want to tell or learn more about within your area of specialization?

Fact, not fiction

God hath framed the mind of man as a mirror or glass, capable of the image of the universal world.

Francis Bacon, *The Advancement of Learning*

The two related ideas, *fact* and *fiction*, are easily understood in common, everyday English conversation. Unfortunately, the distinction between fact and fiction becomes complicated in academic practice. The importance placed on research methods derives from the practical concerns of making this distinction.

Deciding between fact and fiction is often simple and obvious, and so it is easy to develop an unconscious pattern of reasoning in terms of clear-cut right and wrong. It's a very practical way of thinking, and almost impossible to escape. Many or most situations in everyday life can be understood in this way: if you forget where you parked your car in a huge parking lot and the person who accompanied you says, "it's in section D4," you can easily check whether that is true or false. If you wonder whether you remembered to put the groceries away after getting home from the market, it's easy to tell whether or not you have.[3] When a newspaper writer quotes from a recorded speech by a public figure, the quotation can be checked against the recording for accuracy. In these and many other everyday situations, it's easy to say *true* or *false*. Years of schooling can tend to reinforce a clear dichotomy between true and false, correct and incorrect, and fact and fiction. But analyzing and interpreting data are not always so clear-cut, nor is the choice between two competing theories in the literature.

When considering a research question, a basic intuition of right and wrong is a crucial contributor to the reasoning process—such intuition can guide interpretation of difficult material or evidence. Research aims to identify the "right" explanation—the fact—not the "wrong"—the fiction.

This sense of right versus wrong is a powerful motivator and guide. It can direct the development of hypotheses for testing, and the discovery of questions to explore. Without such a sense of right and wrong, it's pretty easy to get lost in debates and doubt, because logical certainty can be elusive.

As scholars move from their internal, personal choice between "right" and "wrong" into a more public sphere—when they present work to others—that choice will be acceptable as research if it meets the standards of their community, or at least as those standards are interpreted by individual readers/reviewers. The research in peer-reviewed journals has been accepted by reviewers who judge the work according to their personal standards. Your work, too, will need to be accepted by some reviewers. When reading the literature in your field, you want to look for the ways in which the accepted scholarship argues for its validity (and the limits thereof). And when writing your own research, you want to use similar steps to argue for the validity of your work.

Some manner of differentiating between "fact" and "fiction" is necessary for the community. Scholars cannot just make up stories or invent data. Therefore, although an intuitive sense of right and wrong is an invaluable and necessary tool for a scholar, it is not enough. When someone asks "How do you know that?," answering "It's my intuition" won't usually satisfy the questioner (especially if they are a professor and you are a student seeking their signature on a thesis or dissertation). To work in their community, scholars need to be able to explain their reasoning and to give explanations that satisfy community conventions.

The main way that research separates fact from fiction is to follow appropriate methods.[4] But someone trying to design and propose a project doesn't necessarily know which methods are most appropriate, nor, for that matter, what question is most appropriate. With such doubt, how is a research designer supposed to demonstrate that a research plan is well-founded? In most research communities the answer is to cite another source. Once a work has been accepted by the community, its claims are given greater credibility. Published research is generally accepted as sufficiently sound as to serve as the foundation for future research. For this reason, the design of research projects depends on reading and writing about the published literature. This is good, because it's necessary to have something strong on which to build your research. This is bad, because the literature is filled with debates and disagreements, and it can be difficult to make decisions about which side of a dispute has the stronger position.

It would be great if research had clear and certain distinctions between fact and fiction, but real research doesn't match the ideal. Real research doesn't produce certainty, though it may produce confidence. But still, it strives to deal in fact, not fiction, and to set foundations for research that is valuable to a whole community.

Exercises (5 to 10 minutes each)

Do you believe in "facts"? Why or why not?

Do you believe that some things are true for all people? Examples?

If there are no "facts," what can research tell us?

Does your view of "facts" agree with scholars in your community? What are the differences between your views and those of some scholars in your field?

Uncertainty

> The Tao that can be spoken is not the eternal Tao [or, taking some liberty with translation, "The truth that can be put into words is not the ultimate truth."]
>
> Lao Tzu, *Tao Te Ching*, verse 1

One thing is certain about research: there will be uncertainty. There may be some moments of certainty—mathematical proofs, for example—but on the whole, there will be uncertainty. In his book *The Logic of Scientific Discovery*, the philosopher Karl Popper[5] wrote: "Science is not a system of certain, or well-established, statements; nor is it a system which steadily advances towards a state of finality."[6]

Uncertainty, of course, is what motivates research—research hopes to transform the unknown to the known. Without questions and doubt, there is no research.

Unfortunately, however, research does not dispel all uncertainty. As Popper says about science, research does not advance toward a state of finality. A lot of research makes its uncertainty explicit by writing about limitations and suggestions for future research.

Practically speaking, if you want to find doubt in research, there are plenty of places to look. All research rests on premises that can be challenged.

Definitions used to guide research can be challenged. One can often find that some relevant factor hasn't been taken into account, or that a significant implication of the data or the model has not been considered. The literature is filled with—even built upon—claims that previous research wasn't good enough. In the influential model of science proposed by Popper, one major role of the scientific community is to test hypotheses that have not yet been disproven, or, in other words, to challenge ideas that are accepted.

For the research designer, the uncertainty presents an opportunity and also a danger. Uncertainty presents opportunity for a researcher because where there is uncertainty, there are questions to be answered by research. The danger is that questions proliferate more quickly than answers, and the research designer needs to commit to a single question.

To design a research project, it is important to be able to recognize the uncertainties that are present in the work of others, and to see how to work with them. On the first point, recognizing uncertainty in something you're reading can provide opportunities to develop your own research—those uncertainties are the proverbial "gaps in the literature" for research to address. On the second, recognizing the uncertainties lets you see how other authors manage them, providing a good model for dealing with similar uncertainties in your own work—not to mention a measure of confidence that comes with recognizing that other works also have uncertainties.

For some scholars, uncertainty is so fundamental to research that it is accepted almost beyond question. Research using inferential statistics relies on probability not certainty: statistical tests that discuss a p value all depend on the idea that a result is unlikely to have happened by chance. Whether the p value is set to 0.5 (one in twenty) or 0.0001 (one in ten thousand), the conclusion is based on likelihood, not certainty. Similarly, scholars who rely on any of the wide range of philosophies that reject objective truth—for example, post-modern philosophies or American Pragmatism—all proceed without logical certainty, often focusing on the active aspect of their work rather than the expository (e.g., the Pragmatists expressed interest not in the "truth value" of an idea but in its "cash value," i.e., how that idea played out when put into action).

Whatever your philosophical position, it is important to recognize the uncertainty that exists in academic debates: logically speaking, there are always questions that could be asked. This uncertainty fuels scholarly debate in your field, so it's useful if you're looking for research opportunities. But it's also a danger, especially to the cautious or skeptical: if you doubt everything, you become paralyzed.

Exercises (30 to 60 seconds, repeat for 10 to 20 minutes)

List ideas that you doubt, but that most people accept.

List ideas that you believe, but that most people reject.

The community of researchers

I ended the last section by suggesting that uncertainty is rife, and with a caution of the danger of doubting everything. How do we stop doubting? From a purely logical perspective, we don't. The theoretical response to this logical gap is to look to practice. Pragmatically, we use the best theory we have, even though it may be proven wrong at some time in the future. And how do we recognize the best theory if we can't prove it true? This is where community comes into the picture.

To describe the role of community, I am going to go as deep into philosophy as I will get in this book. If you don't care about the philosophical foundations, then you might reasonably choose to skip this section, taking away only this: 1) research develops within a community of researchers seeking to develop the communal understanding of a subject, and 2) research literature is the written record of the exchange of ideas (i.e., a conversation) among the researchers in the field.

The question of whether or not there is any objective truth is, and has long been, widely debated. It's not a question with which I want to engage. For the purposes of this book, I encourage you to consider what you believe on the matter—is there objective truth? If not, what are you doing as a researcher? And consider: how does your view of research compare to the views of your professors and fellow students? To the people whose work you read?

This crucial role for community forces research into practical dimensions: research isn't just ideas, it's ideas that need to be communicated and discussed in a community.

Drawing conclusions from observations: empiricism and the process of induction

The most basic concern of research is the use of evidence: researchers gather data—evidence—which is used in developing and testing theories. But logical problems arise from the attempt to use evidence. (These next paragraphs are as deep in philosophy as I get.)

To some extent, we all automatically draw conclusions from evidence—from prior experience—and use that evidence to form expectations about the future. If we try some new food and enjoy it, we are inclined to believe that we will enjoy that same food in the future. If we enjoy some food several times, our assumption that we will enjoy it in the future is strengthened. The process of making a generalization from experience is known as the process of induction.

Empirical science operates on this basic principle: it gathers data and makes general rules from those data. A researcher who sets up an experiment typically does so in such a way that the experiment is replicable so that someone else doing the same experiment will get the same (or extremely similar) results. The basic notion is that observed patterns of behavior (whether the behavior of some sub-atomic particle, or some biological process, or some social pattern, etc.) will be repeated in the future. If you study in a field that gathers data to be used as evidence in your arguments—which is to say most university departments—then you're likely to be dealing with this basic pattern.

Unfortunately, the process of induction has a problem. In the 18th century, the philosopher David Hume famously argued that we cannot assume that the future will resemble the past. Just because we have, for example, observed thousands or millions of swans, all of which are white, we cannot therefore assume that the next swan we see will also be white. Hume's argument against the certainty of induction inspired many who wished for greater certainty. Immanuel Kant explicitly credits Hume's work on this issue for "interrupting" his "dogmatic slumbers,"[7] thereby leading him into his great works. Karl Popper, mentioned above, was also spurred by Hume in his examination of the role of induction in science—he frequently called the problem of induction, "Hume's problem."

Popper's basic argument for objective knowledge is that, although we cannot prove that anything is true because some future observation might contradict the observations we have made so far, we can prove that something is false for a certainty. For example, the claim that all swans are white is absolutely disproven by the existence of a black swan. So, although we cannot know with certainty when we are right (we cannot prove that a claim is true), we can know with certainty when we are wrong (because we can prove that a claim is false).

This led Popper to the conclusion that science proceeded through a process of falsification—of generating, testing, and rejecting hypotheses. His basic argument focuses on questions of logical proof: the idea that we can prove absolutely that a claim is false provides a claim to the desired "objective truth." But underlying the focus on logical concerns is an implicit social process: who tests hypotheses? A community of scholars. Although Popper's model claims objective knowledge, that is limited to knowledge of what is false. For what is accepted as true, Popper suggests using a "best-tested theory," but such a status depends on the behavior of a research community to carry out tests.

To develop your own research and use research literature effectively, it is crucial to understand how the entire fabric of academic work is a set of interweaving ideas, all of which are open to debate both logically speaking, and literally speaking, in the case of any issue disputed in the published literature.

All the scholarly literature that you read, as well as what you write, is embedded in this community. The literature—the written record of the community—is a touchstone for helping researchers identify ideas that need testing and for guiding the community effort in search of greater understanding. The literature is the formal record of the debates among scholars on the questions that they study. Your research is an entry into that debate, and so should understand and speak the language of that community and act in a manner consistent with the community's standards for research behavior.

Exercises (10 to 20 minutes, total)

What communities of scholars are important to you? To what communities do you belong? Your department, and what else? Any groups within your department? Groups of friends interested in a similar question? Formal working groups? What about outside your department? Are there any larger groups to which you feel attached? If you identify as a "social scientist," that would be one overarching definition that encompasses many different university departments. Or, for example, "qualitative researchers" might be a community to which you belong.

With whom would you like to be in a community?

Are there any people in any of your communities that you don't want to be in a community with?

The research literature: a conversation among scholars

As a student doing coursework, you read scholarly literature to find the "truth" contained therein, or maybe, more cynically, to find the "truth" you thought your professor wanted you to find. When you're reading material assigned for a course, there is usually a specific concern that your professor would like you to recognize and discuss. But as an independent researcher you look at each publication for what it offers you: is it a potential tool? Does it guide or support your own entry into the large, diverse conversation among researchers in your field?

Each piece you read—every book, every article, every essay—is part of a larger conversation. Sometimes this conversational nature is very explicit, with authors saying, "this work was inspired by ...," as Kant and Popper did in response to David Hume. Other times, authors will keep the focus on specific issues or premises, but even in such cases, these premises will align with ideas expressed by others. Whether explicitly addressing a person, or addressing an abstract idea, as soon as you structure a question based on what you have learned, you are implicitly responding to what others have said.[8]

For one person to be intelligible to another requires at least some shared perspective—a shared language of some sort, and at least some shared ideas. Because the questions and ideas that people use are inevitably shaped by their context and their experience, and people's context includes other people, everyone is sharing in and being shaped by this conversation, whether or not they are conscious of it, or conscious of its conversational nature.[9] For scholars, even if many of their ideas about their own field are novel, the very idea of scholarship and/or research itself provides a context of shared ideas that shapes the work. And to work within a field of study requires a set of premises shared with other scholars—some sense of common purpose—even if the questions the scholar is examining within that field are not common among other researchers. Even if the scholar thinks to him or herself, "All of these other people are going about X the wrong way," that thought has an implicit comparison that reveals the shared ground, and the conversation he or she would have with them: "You guys have all done X this way, but it's much better to do X that way!"[10] Whatever X may be, it is the shared ground.

In the simplistic view of research where works are judged "true," any "truth" is the end of a road: one does not need to examine or discuss beyond these points. With a richer view—seeing the literature as a dialogue among individuals seeking a shared understanding—you start to compare each author's ideas with those of others, and can thereby see their imperfections more clearly. Seeing the repeated attempts to define and describe an idea, and seeing the slight variations in these different definitions and descriptions, leads to asking not whether a statement is true or false, but how the ideas in the statement work; themselves and together with other ideas in the literature. In addition to considering whether you agree, you can look to see how others have built ideas, and how each individual entry into the discussion works with and against the other works and how the different expressions of the same idea interact with each other (both in agreement and in conflict) in the fabric of the field's discourse. With this vision, the scholar does not try to present certain, proven ideas, but rather shows how their own work builds on and fits into the larger framework of varied ideas that makes up the scholarly discourse in the field.

Ultimately, when performing research, you will develop your own questions from the fabric of the discourse that has preceded you. Originality comes from challenging some, but not all, aspects of this discourse. Even original thinkers are mostly working within the framework created by the larger conversation going on in the world around them. All researchers—whether giants like Sir Isaac Newton or just modest contributors—see farther by standing on the shoulders of those who have preceded them.

If you think of what you do as "research," and you are doing it within a research institution (e.g., a university), then you are part of the discourse of that institution and that community, and you are expected to meet certain criteria of scholarship to be taken seriously by those who make up the institution. You can expect, for example, that most researchers at most research institutions, along with editors at academic publishers, will want empirical evidence and will reject an assertion founded on a claim of divine inspiration. To get other scholars to take you seriously, you have to speak their language and use their type of reasoning. To be a researcher in a research institution depends on some shared understanding with the rest of the community. That sharing is built through communication.

The rest of this book depends on this perspective of research as a large-scale conversation among scholars: when you are thinking about research literature —both that of other researchers, and the work that you are writing—think of how it grew out of a community of people working together to define and explain some set of phenomena. All researchers—you included—are working with other researchers in search of an understanding that can be shared. By understanding how other researchers fit their work into the discourse of your research community, you, too, can fit your work into that same conversation.

Exercises (15 to 30 minutes)

(Thought experiment from above): What would happen if you submitted a paper that said "I know this is true because I was divinely inspired"? Who would accept that paper? Who would reject it? What reasons would be given for acceptance or rejection?

Identify and write about some of the disagreements that you have seen in literature—who contradicts whom? Who agrees with whom?

Project 1: what does research do for you?

What is important to you? The clearer your sense of purpose, the easier it is to design a research project. If your sense of purpose isn't clear, this is an opportunity to explore ideas to find something you feel important and worth your effort.

Here you are asked to explicate your purpose in carrying out your research project. It also gives you practice in writing a type of written work that you're often called upon to write: a brief statement of purpose for a project.

Step 1: Write a brief description of the purposes of an independent research project.

Write one or two sentences on each of the following points:

- What is the general subject or concern?
- Why is it important?
- What is the specific research question and what do you hope to find?
- Why is that important?
- What kinds of data will you gather and what kinds of analysis will you use?
- Who would be interested in this research and why would they be interested in it?

The total should be no more than 200 words.

Step 2: Set aside the first draft and write a second draft starting from a blank page.

Step 3: Edit and proofread.

Writing can take a lot of time if you look for the perfect word. Instead of looking for the best phrases, write quickly and experiment. Try using one possibility and seeing where that leads instead of musing over the choice.

Post-project evaluation: How much variation was there between the two drafts? How much time did you spend? Would spending more time significantly improve the drafts you wrote?

Notes

1 In Plato's dialogues, Socrates is frequently asserting how little he knows as the basis for his questions that then reveal how limited the knowledge of his interlocutor.
2 And others, if you're ready for feedback.
3 It's possible, of course, to put some of the groceries away, but not all, in which case you both have and have not put the groceries away—so this question isn't quite so simple, actually. The process of research can be a little like this: first you say "it's simple," but then you see some complexity that arises.

4 Research methods are crucial to research for their place in the attempt to separate fact from fiction. Discussing the benefit of methods, however, is a matter for another work. This book is concerned with the parts of research that cannot be addressed with methods.

5 Popper's model for science was one of the dominant models of science through the 20th century. It is discussed in greater detail in the next section.

6 Popper, *Logic of Scientific Discovery*, Chapter 10. Routledge Classics, 2002, p.278.

7 *Prolegomena to Any Future Metaphysics* (1783).

8 If you address a point that no-one has previously discussed, that, too, is a response to what has been said. Saying "this research addresses a point that has not been previously researched," is equivalent to saying "no-one has talked about this point so far."

9 A student who learns, e.g., the theory of heliocentric universe (or solar system, at least), and accepts it, may think of that theory as a set truth, and not as part of a larger theoretical conversation, but that theory, historically speaking, is only one voice in a larger theoretical conversation. Today, that conversation is mostly beyond debate, but still, there are flat-earthers who express their doubts.

10 So, for example, a literary critic may look at another work of literary criticism and say "they're going about it all wrong," but is unlikely to look at a work of particle physics and make the same claim. And the physicist is going to critique research in physics, not works in literary criticism. (Or at least not in the course of their own research. Although no physicist is going to use laboratory resources to debate Judith Butler, one might, for fun, write and submit a mock post-modern work as a hoax. Indeed, physicist Alan Sokal did precisely this in the 1990s.)

Research practice

Research is not just an abstract intellectual attempt to separate fact from fiction or to tell an evidence-based story about the world. It has practical dimensions. It is an activity or series of activities: you acquire and read source materials, you think about how to use those materials and how to develop your research project (thinking is an activity!), you write about your work—all of these are activities. All of these require time and effort, and possibly other resources as well. These practical dimensions are crucial—time, especially. Wouldn't it be better to finish your dissertation and get your degree in a timely fashion?

At stake here is a vision of the research process. Do we imagine the researcher single-mindedly pursuing a method to a goal, or do we imagine the researcher exploring and experimenting, taking chances and making mistakes? If the whole of research is method, then you follow a method to the end, and if you make mistakes, you start again, with the previous effort wasted. But if research is a practice, you do your best, and you learn along the way, refining not only your project, but also your abilities as a researcher.

When discussing the value of practice, there is a useful analogy between being a good researcher and being a good cook. The researcher and the cook both want to produce a good product—the researcher, research; the cook, food. Both can rely on methods: research methods for the researcher, recipes for the cook.

But being a good cook requires more than just good recipes, and this is where the skill and judgment of experience come in. First of all, a recipe is not the same to all cooks: for a chef, it may lead to a feast, while for a novice cook it may lead to an inedible mess. The difference lies in the subtle differences in experience and skill: the expert is better able to manage any number of fine details, from selection of better quality ingredients, to greater facility with knives and other utensils, to better judgment of the right levels of heat, to adaptations required by context (for example, substituting an ingredient, if necessary). The experienced cook has skills that make the whole process of following a recipe more successful (and possibly more enjoyable, as well). Additionally, their skills help them identify different situations in which different recipes might be better. Similarly, the experienced researcher will be better able to choose appropriate methods, make necessary adjustments in research design to deal with contextual concerns, and deal with other difficulties in the process.

I don't want to push this analogy too far. It could be argued that this analogy fails because of a big practical difference: a cook's recipes take only hours, and a cook can practice multiple recipes in a day. By contrast, a significant research project could take a year or more, and a researcher can't possibly do several projects just to build up skills. But in practice, a big project is manifested through a series of smaller projects. A dissertation (or book or journal article) is only the final product of an extended process requiring numerous pieces of writing, including some or all of the following: a prospectus at the very beginning, a formal proposal, a proposal to an IRB, applications for grants/fellowships, departmental progress reports, e-mails with professors, conversations with professors, presentations in seminars (and perhaps other communications)—not to mention the drafts of the final manuscript. It will also include various data-gathering projects, including a long series of readings. It may also include a number of oral presentations of your work. Each written submission, spoken presentation, or other task is a little project in its own right. In this view, the draft that you submit to your professor is not *The Project*, but rather just another test recipe on the road to a final project.

To some extent, then, this book argues that in order to finish your dissertation, you should become an expert researcher, and the necessary work will be produced as you experiment and explore your subject of interest, and as you try to define and refine your own research project. This chapter discusses the development of a practice.

Your vision, your purposes

If you are seeking an advanced degree, then you are already looking toward a career in which you are an expert of some sort. Academics become teachers and researchers, of course. But professionals, too, become experts. The clinician provides expertise as a practitioner: working with individual cases and making important decisions about how to proceed. The educator, too, is providing expertise; not only to teach a subject, but to apply pedagogical methods.

Central to all of these activities is the ability of the expert practitioner to make a good decision based on what he or she knows at the time the decision must be made. That is what the expert is consulted for, and such decisions require confidence in one's own vision and ability. It requires identifying what you think is important. Research is no different, really: the researcher, too, is an expert who is making decisions about how to develop projects to answer questions in the theoretical discourse.

When it comes to developing your own vision and your own judgment, use of methods can be constraining in negative ways. I want to reiterate the great value of methods—research is much better for them. Methods help protect against all sorts of errors that plague empirical research. But there are times when methods don't help, and even times when methods are a hindrance.

Methods are set—fixed and determined—which is very good for participation in a community because it provides a structure that people can share. However, depending on a fixed method can inhibit the desired growth of the individual researcher. If you think of research as following a method, you follow that method as best you can to its completion, and then see what the method reveals. If you think of research as a practice for developing skills, then you regularly assess your progress and see what you have learned.

At the large scale, I dislike methods because they can defer responsibility: you can follow the steps of a method without questioning and without self-reflection. That doesn't necessarily help you build the habit of making decisions and developing your own purposes to guide your own practice. Methods are a good support for a research practice, but they are not a good guide to the most important issues.

For research design, you need to develop and refine your own vision and your own purposes, and that takes a willingness to explore, experiment, and make mistakes. That exploratory practice gives you space to learn about different approaches and an opportunity to make choices rather than just following steps prescribed by someone else. If you aspire to be an expert and a decision-maker, then it's important to start practicing making decisions based on your best judgments.

Part of having your own vision is your own sense of purpose, your own sense of what is important and what you are trying to accomplish.

On a broad level, a sense of purpose is crucial for direction and motivation. If you feel like you're just doing something that you've been ordered to do, it's much harder to find motivation than if you're doing something that you believe in. If you're doing a research project because someone said, "that will be an easy project," it can be hard to find motivation, especially if your response was, "OK, I guess." If, however, you think that your project will give you information that matters to you, it's much easier to find motivation.

But on a more fine-grained level, you want to have a sense of purpose for the different tasks that you undertake. If you feel a task is pointless, it's much harder to engage in that task and much harder to do it well. Motivationally, it's a drag doing something meaningless. Functionally, if something seems meaningless, it's hard to do it right because your effort can be misplaced. Along these lines, I had something of a personal epiphany with respect to punctuation in my first semester in graduate school. I had always struggled with punctuation as a bunch of rules my teachers expected me to follow—some sort of task whose only purpose seemed to be to please my teachers. I didn't think of punctuation in terms of its role in helping me communicate with other people until a professor explicitly framed it in terms of getting people to take me seriously, rather than as just satisfying professors. As soon as I shifted my efforts from trying to follow rules of grammar to trying to communicate, it became easier to punctuate—not only did I stop resenting the necessary effort, but the sense of purpose made it easier for me to negotiate those previously problematic rules. Generally, the clearer your sense of purpose, the easier it is to direct your effort effectively.

Different purposes in the research process can influence different kinds of engagement with the literature. One day you might be exploring (looking at a range of different theories of, for example, metaphor), another you might be reading with a more specific question (for example, how metaphor relates to thought), and then, later, you might be looking at an even more specific question (for example, how to analyze a specific metaphor in a specific text, using a specific theory of metaphor). Your purposes will shift as you learn, as you develop your project, and as you focus on the issues that most interest you.

By thinking of research as a practice, you can start to develop a sense of how different actions will help you move your own project forward. The practice may lead to mistakes, but it also leads you to the kind of progress you need to make in developing your own project, and it lays a foundation of skills that will help with other projects in your future.

Exercises (10–20 minutes)

Do you prefer to follow orders or to make decisions for yourself? What are the strengths and weaknesses of following orders? And of making decisions for yourself? How can you get better at following orders? How can you get better at making decisions for yourself?

Allocation of resources

From the practical perspective, we see that research and research design require resources, and resources are scarce. You can't just approach research from the purely intellectual stance of pursuing some question of interest; you have to make your research project work, and you have to do so at a reasonable cost. The same dissertation that would be an excellent project if it took two years would be a terrible project if it took five years and cost the writer his or her health.

Time and money, obviously, are basic resources expended. Additionally, your health is a resource that can impact and be impacted by your practices as a researcher. Your family relationships are a resource that can impact and be impacted by your practices. So, too, are your professional relationships. Your research design decisions impact your resources, so they are consequential—mistakes have a real cost—and at the same time your decisions are made in the face of uncertainty: you can't be certain that your plan will work out!

All of these resources demand attention in the process of research design with respect to the project you plan. From this perspective, the concern of a researcher is for project management: the project that you design should be something that can be accomplished in a reasonable time and with reasonable effort.

Furthermore, it's worth keeping in mind that the very process of research design also takes resources. If you're not careful, research design can take a big chunk of time. Research design doesn't offer clear answers as to what the best project is, and any choice is important because of the resource costs. This can lead to doubt and a string of project ideas that follow each other in succession without ever coalescing into a specific research plan and proposal that you can carry out. Trying to review a lot of different literature in the research design phase, especially with an eye toward learning new ideas, can eat up a lot of resources while leading only to uncertainty. A willingness to take a chance and be wrong is crucial in getting through the research design process, especially with respect to getting feedback on your research design plans.

How much time should you allocate?

What should a dissertation demand of a student? What is a reasonable expectation of time and effort? For a project as a whole, and for the research design of the project? There is some variation in this, but I think it hardly out of the question to say that five years should be a reasonable upper limit: if a student spends more than five years, that's a problem. So five years is an upper limit. What is a minimum time allocation suitable? Perhaps a year? That's a pretty optimistic target—it's a target that is possible if everything goes right, if you already know what you want to do, and have no troubles designing or executing your project. So, you should probably be thinking in terms of allocating two years, roughly. If you develop a regular research practice and spend some time working on your project most days, there's a good chance that two years will be more than enough.

Resources allocated for skill-building

The idea of building skills through practice can be intimidating because skills are often slow to develop. If you invest effort in skill-building, will it be worth it? The precise measure of "is it worth it?" is difficult. I believe it is worth it, and I believe it is worth it in the context of a single research project.

Building skills is valuable in the long run: developing skill as a writer, especially, will aid you in any professional or academic career. Being able to write quickly and effectively is a valuable skill, unlikely to go out of style. The skills of a researcher and research designer—the ability to gather information, to process it into useful conclusions—those are also valuable skills in any career where you aspire to be a lead decision-maker.

But even just looking to the end of the dissertation, still, the skill-building path is the best way to proceed. If you're looking at a dissertation timeline of a year or more, that is plenty of time to develop skills, but I think the issue isn't so much the need to develop skills—most graduate students have plenty of skills—as it is to start to use them effectively. By thinking about your practice building your skills, you can worry less about immediate difficulties and keep your eyes on the longer goal of developing your own vision, voice, story, and research project.

Exercises (15 minutes)

How long do you want to spend on your research project?

How long do you think you will spend?

How long have you spent?

Are there other resources (aside from your time and effort) that you can use to help in your project? That you would want to use to help in your project?

How long should you spend designing a project before you propose it?

How much time should you spend on reviewing literature before you start designing your own project?

Research design

Research literature—the public face of research, so to speak—presents the final conclusion of a research project. It shows a set of motivating questions, methods, results, and conclusions drawn from the results. It shows what a project looks like when it's finished. It doesn't necessarily show you how the project moved from inception to completion or the difficulties that the authors faced. And it will rarely focus attention on issues that other scholars might consider fatal intellectual flaws: authors show belief in their own work, and don't spend their time talking about all the potential arguments against their work. The literature reveals many important things, but it does not reveal the difficulties of research design.

For the independent researcher, designing a good project is the necessary preliminary to completing a project, and it is very difficult. Designing a research project requires you to be able to handle the theoretical complexities in your field, certainly, but it also involves other considerations of no small significance. For example, your choice of topic will influence not only the professors with whom you work while in school, but also the shape of your future career. Your choice of a theoretical foundation and method will also influence the people you work with and who supports or rejects your work. These social and political dimensions of research have significant practical impact. Choices of topic, theory, and method also shape the resources you need to carry out your research. Some data will cost a lot more in time and money to generate than others. Few (or none) of these choices have clear answers. They often involve trade-offs: for example, what if the project that most interests you means working with a difficult professor, or choosing a more difficult career path?

It is common to talk about defining a question (or a topic or a problem) as the first step in the research process. A common simplified description of research is: define a question; gather data; analyze the data; report the data. Unfortunately, defining a good question *can be* difficult for many reasons. I emphasize the words "can be" because it is an area where experience is extremely valuable. An experienced researcher who has already defined and completed many research projects may find it quite easy to define a new project.[1] Experienced researchers already know what has and hasn't worked in their past, which helps them make good choices. They can make good assessments of how difficult it will be to gather and analyze data. Their methods, instruments, and equipment are already familiar. They have a sense of which problems they can work through, and which to avoid completely. They may have a social network of other researchers who can provide feedback. And, perhaps most crucially, they have the confidence of having done it all before.[2]

One of the biggest difficulties for inexperienced independent researchers is getting past the self-doubt. To design your own project, you need to believe that your own ideas—your own voice and vision—have a worthy place in the conversation, and that belief has to be strong enough to carry you through any difficulties that might arise. You need to believe that you add something to the discourse in your field.

Many begin the process of research design with the entirely reasonable step of performing a review of literature on their topic of interest. But without a strong focus on the need to define a project you can complete—if you read with too great a willingness to try new ideas—this process can lead you in an ever-expanding search for the answers found by other people, and keep you from developing your own project and your own answers.

As you engage the literature while designing a project for your dissertation or thesis, you are not following a fixed recipe that leads to a known destination, but rather beginning a process of exploration in which you will improve your knowledge, your scholarly skills, and your sense of what you want to study and how to study it.

The research literature, the record of the research done by others in your field, contains not only a theoretical debate, but also evidence of how other researchers approached their work, how they asked questions, how they chose methods and subjects, how they dealt with the weaknesses of their work, and other issues of import to research design.

When you engage the process of reviewing literature during research design, it may be more productive to think of each new day's work as a new attempt to design a good research project, and the reading you do that day as a guide to designing a suitable project.

If you are a graduate student beginning a dissertation or thesis, your crucial task is to design your own research project. To this end, you use the literature to help you develop your own voice and vision, not simply to absorb what others have written.

Exercises (5 minutes, repeat a few times)

Describe a research project you think you could carry out to completion. What is the research question? What is the research method? What is one source that inspired the project? Be brief. Limit your response to a few sentences.

Try to describe a few different projects in this way.

Defining the research question is a significant problem

One of the most consequential and difficult decisions facing a researcher is deciding which question to research. It's consequential because it will shape the kind of work you do and the people with whom you will work for the immediate future, and perhaps in the long run, too. It's difficult because of all the uncertainties involved.

There is a huge gap between the kind of question that motivates a researcher—a desire to understand or explain some general phenomenon—and the kind of question that works for a research project. The first kind of question, a motivating question, typically encompasses too much material to support a clear, focused analysis of research data.

Here are some questions that might be motivating questions, but would be too general for most research projects:

- How can we improve health outcomes for individuals with a specific disease, condition, or diagnosis?
- How can management improve performance of workers (in a given field)?
- How can teachers improve performance of students in a given area of study (e.g., STEM, Language, Arts), in a given age group (e.g., elementary students, secondary students), or in a given educational context (e.g., in schools without sufficient funding; in schools limited by some specific policy, like the US "No Child Left Behind" or "Common Core" standards)?
- How are members of a certain population impacted by a specific policy (e.g., how are children born in the US to parents who are illegal immigrants affected by policies to detain or deport illegal aliens, or how are students with learning disabilities affected by educational policies)?

Such questions are so complex that they exceed the practical scope of any single research study. The complexity here becomes apparent with only a little attention to detail or variation. For example, in the first topic above—improving outcomes for ailing individuals—significant variation might be expected between different groups of people (e.g., women vs. men; children vs. adults; wealthy vs. poor; etc.) and between different aspects of outcomes (e.g., physiological and psychological), and each of these variations might call for a different kind of research. To answer questions about psychological outcomes, for example, requires different tools and methods than to answer questions about physiological outcomes.

In the second and third topics—improving worker performance and student performance—there are different aspects and measures of performance and different types of interventions that could be tested, each of which could generate a separate study.

In the fourth topic—impact of policy on populations—there are multiple dimensions of impact (e.g., economic, social, psychological). For each dimension, there are different methods of assessing the outcome, and each method calls for a research project with certain requirements.

One reason mixed-methods studies are so common and valuable is that they start to address the multi-dimensionality in a subject of study. But, practically speaking, mixed-methods studies require more resources. At a minimum, there are two complete data collection efforts that must each be designed and carried out. Further, adding an additional research modality may introduce additional theoretical concerns.[3]

General questions about important issues, like those listed above, can require significant effort and skill to refine into a research project that is both worthwhile and practical, given your available resources.

To find a question in which theory, method, and practical empirical concerns (i.e., issues of data gathering and analysis) all align is not a trivial effort, especially for people who have never designed or executed an independent research project. Exploring different questions can help, as can efforts to refine a current question.

In any event, if you have difficulty defining a good question, that is not some personal failing, but rather the nature of the beast.

Exercises (Five repetitions, 2.5 minutes each)

First, record a spoken version of your research question in under 30 seconds (what might be called the "elevator pitch" of your question).

Then, write a version of that recorded question in 2 minutes or less.

Repeat, trying different phrasing and focus.

The problem of learning

One of the big difficulties with research design, and especially with reviewing literature in the process of research design, is how much you learn. Learning might not seem like a problem—Learning is good! It's why we do research!—but learning can be a problem in the practical context of research design and completing a research project. Learning changes how you see the world, and particularly how you see the subject you're studying. Such changes can shift your views of what would make a good project, sometimes in drastic ways: more than one dissertation writer has decided that their whole project needs to be re-started.

For all the benefit of learning, new ideas pose a great danger to the design and completion of a research project (or a writing project, or, really, any other project). Research design requires a commitment to specific ideas, and discovery of new ideas often works against that commitment. Near the beginning of a project, too much reading can prevent making the initial commitments necessary to advance, and you can get stuck saying, "I still have to read more," or writing excessively long literature reviews that still don't work for you.

The danger does not pass with the initial commitment: having gotten deep into the project, you may well come across a difficulty that you had not anticipated and, at the same time, you can clearly imagine a good alternative to your current project that resolves the current problem. At such a moment, it can be very tempting to put aside the current project with its current difficulties in favor of the apparently excellent new possibility.

Early in the process, it's good to have some openness to learning and to change, and even late in the process, it's important to be able to make big changes if there are truly insurmountable problems. But, to finish a project, you need to be able to commit to what you started, even though you see it as flawed.

Viewing your work as a practice can make it easier to finish out a flawed project. If you are following a method, and feel that you have failed the method in some way, then, from a purely logical perspective, there's no real point in continuing because it is only the method that separates acceptable work from unacceptable. But if all research is flawed, the point of continuing is, on the personal level, to develop experience and skill, and on the community level, to contribute to the community by sharing what you learned from your earlier mistakes and the new questions that you would ask if starting a project today.

On the personal level, the skills you develop are those of being able to recognize subtle distinctions in the relationship between theory and appropriate research methods. To reuse the cooking analogy, the practice is trying the same recipe, day after day, with a willingness to get it wrong early in the process to ensure good outcomes later in the process. With the practice comes a finer sensitivity to important issues: an experienced cook might have a more discerning palate than the novice, for example. Performing artists might similarly use early rehearsals to explore possibilities with less concern for getting it right, and more concern for being able to do it well later. Similarly, a researcher might develop abilities to analyze their subject and to apply research methods in effective ways. This learning is valuable, but the practitioner also needs to produce a work shared with the public—the chef, a meal; the performer, a performance; and the researcher, a dissertation or publication.

In your practice, you want to be able to learn and grow. If you're just starting a research project, it may be worth doing some exploratory reading, looking for new ideas, but exploratory reading is something most graduate students have plenty of experience with. Too many new ideas can inhibit developing a single research project.

Exercises (10 minutes)

What new ideas have you learned recently? Did any of those ideas influence what you think a good research project would be? How did your research project change?

Use what you already know

In response to the problem of learning and the concern for limited resources, try to build your practice on what you already do know, and make sure to use what you already do know and what you already believe.

In my experience, it's common for students embarking on their dissertation to think something along the lines of, "I don't really know what's going on; I'm just starting this." There's a pleasant humility to this, but it's not for the best, I think.[4] Claiming ignorance discounts all the education that brought you to where you are—and, realistically, if you are working on a graduate degree, you are highly educated already. It is unusual for a student to advance to doing independent graduate research without a very good idea of what is going on. Nonetheless, it is pretty common for students to get stuck saying, "I don't know enough; I just need to read a few more articles before I start." To avoid getting stuck focusing on all you don't know, focus on what you do know.

Many scholars struggle to make explicit their intellectual foundations. In particular, many struggling graduate students keep a gap between their own ideas and the ideas they read in the literature, as if their own ideas are not worthy to be part of the discussion. But the whole point of doing independent research is to test the value of your own ideas in contrast with ideas published in the literature, so it's crucial to make your own ideas and beliefs explicit and see where they take you, rather than just seeking someone else's.

If you want to design your own project and make the necessary commitments, you must, at some point, stop putting energy into learning new ideas, and start putting energy into working with the material you already know. Many scholars decide that they need to read more to find a theory when they would be better served by trying to make explicit their own ideas and the relationship between those ideas and material they have read (or heard from professors or other scholars) in the past.

Working with the material you already know entails both the intellectual dimension of working through ideas, and the communicative dimension of writing the ideas down.

Developing a clear understanding of your own conceptual foundations and being able to make them explicit are crucial steps to developing and completing research projects. If you can use resources that you already have (i.e., the knowledge that you've already gained over your course of study in graduate school), then you don't need to read as much new material. And for that matter, if you can't or don't use past readings effectively, then reading more won't really help.[5]

So, what are the resources that you already have? You may be explicitly aware of how some of your ideas relate to ideas in the literature, but it's also likely that there are ideas that you use almost automatically—without explicit reference to any literature—that could be connected with published literature. For example, people may take for granted various physical laws—e.g., every action has an equal and opposite reaction—without consciously thinking about how Newton first stated them. People who, in discussing other people, use terms and concepts like "id," "ego," and "superego," are using ideas made common by Freud, perhaps without consciously thinking about citing Freud. To the extent that you have ever absorbed, understood, accepted, and used ideas that you learned from a professor or from assigned readings, you have almost certainly used concepts that could be cited without necessarily thinking about those ideas as citable or knowing whom to cite.

What do you think? How do you see the world? You, the scholar, are already imbued with the ideas from the scholarly discourse. Your education up to this point has shaped how you see the world—even if you do not consciously recognize specific influences behind what you learned in earlier study, those ideas were all shaped by the scholarly discourse. If you are working on a graduate degree, you have a lot of knowledge, but you have to trust that knowledge and understand where it came from and how it relates to what other people say: where do you agree and disagree with the published literature that you read?

If you're saying, "I need to read more; I'm not ready to start writing," then you would probably get more benefit from writing about your own ideas than from doing more reading. What do you think? Make it explicit.

Put it on the page and see what you do know and where you have questions. And then look at how the literature supports or contradicts those ideas.

There is a lot that you don't know. No matter what you do, there will still be a lot that you don't know. If you focus on what you don't know, you can get swallowed up in doubt. If you accept that you will have uncertainty, you can devote more attention to building up what you do know. One of the worst traps for a scholar is to focus on thinking, "I don't know enough." Of course you don't. Neither do I. Neither does anyone else. If we knew enough, we wouldn't want or need to do research. Start with what you do know. And if you're looking for something to read, consider whether you might benefit from re-reading something important to you.

Exercises (30 seconds, repeat for 5+ minutes)

Name a course you have taken. Write down an idea you learned in that course. Did you agree or disagree?

Writing and thinking

If you want to use what you already know, it is important to know what you already know, and that may not be trivial. Trying to write out your own ideas is not easy! Being able to make your ideas explicit in writing is a valuable practice for a scholar. Writing is often difficult and frustrating, but it forces a committed engagement with the ideas in a way unlike simple cogitation and rumination: ideas in the imagination are fluid; words on the page are static.

It has been argued that writing is thinking (the first place I remember seeing this was in *The Craft of Research*,[6] but I have seen it elsewhere, variously attributed). I like the idea (and mention it) because it is evocative and useful, even though I think it an over-simplification.[7] Writing—the act of putting ideas into words and sentences on a page—forces a very rigorous and careful kind of thinking that is rarely achieved otherwise.[8] Until you write, it is easy to hold open multiple possibilities. When you put words on the page, you have to make a commitment to specific formulations and interpretations, and that commitment made visible on the page inspires a closer scrutiny than in the process of abstract cogitation. This process of commitment can be very difficult. When it leads to reconsideration of earlier assumptions, it can inspire a researcher to completely change a research project—a double-edged sword in that the new research design may suit needs better, but may also create a significant delay in completing a project.

The commitments a writer must make are often compromises: they are imperfect, perhaps problematic in some ways, but they're also necessary if you want to complete a project. Given the influence of writing on thinking, it is useful to do some writing for the sole purpose of helping you clarify your own thoughts. As a practice, such writing can be free of concerns like grammar and spelling because the point is not so much what you write, as it is what that process does for your thinking. You can write about your own research for the purpose of developing your own understanding, without worrying whether others will approve of either the writing or the reasoning. It can be useful to write to an imagined audience: try to explain the idea to a person, but without any intention of actually giving the writing to anyone.

In the end, you will need to create a final written product to share with others, but not all writing needs to be given away. Some writing is just practice to help explore ideas. What do you think? How does that look to you when you put it in words on the page? What can you learn from the attempt?[9]

Exercises (10 minutes)

Does writing help you clarify ideas? How?

Does writing ever lead you into confusion? How? What happens?

Does it do both?

Practice: writing is a skill to develop

To get better at writing, and at writing about the literature, you have to practice and experiment. Don't write as if each sentence, or paragraph, or draft, is precious. Each sentence, paragraph, or draft is only an attempt to express an idea that might be precious. The ideas are valuable, and it's important to capture them in the most brilliant light. Words that become famous usually do so because they communicate some idea or emotion. Hamlet's query, "to be or not to be," consists of only the simplest words and yet carries weight because it evokes an emotion many have experienced.[10] For a scholar, it's the idea behind the words that matters and finding the right words is not easy.[11]

As a matter of practice, it is possible to approach writing cautiously—to worry about how it will be read by someone else—a professor, a peer, an administrator, etc. With such a mindset, writers sometimes sit and agonize over a single sentence, trying to get it right. Instead, a practice of writing can work toward some of the fluidity that speaking has.

For most people, the process of speaking is pretty fluid, and they can generate comprehensible statements that effectively communicate their ideas to their listeners. There may be hesitations and sentence fragments, but for most people, the process is sufficiently fluid that they focus on what they want to communicate. They don't worry about their grammar, punctuation, or spelling. Try to write with a similar focus on just expressing your ideas without worrying about sentence structure or punctuation. Getting your ideas on the page is the crucial factor in writing. Explore ideas and different ways to express them.

Ironically, if you're concerned with grammar and punctuation, you're more likely to learn to punctuate well by writing a lot of bad sentences than by laboring over one "good" sentence. And you're more likely to turn in well-proofread drafts if you write quickly and leave yourself time to edit. To revisit the cooking metaphor, instead of trying to get a recipe right on the first try, you try the recipe several times to learn what parts are difficult, and where it can be improved.

This book suggests a number of exercises in each chapter, but speaking generally, there are two kinds of writing exercises that I think are crucial in developing your own research project and using the literature effectively: 1) writing about potential research that you might carry out, and 2) writing about how that project compares to the works you read. The key to such writing tasks is to challenge your imagination and your vision of your own project. Even in writing about others, it's in relation to your own work. Practice will help you find the best words to express your own voice.

Writing becomes easier with practice. Or, perhaps, if not easier—writing is a challenge for even accomplished writers—at least your efforts will be rewarded with a superior product.

Exercises (10 minutes)

What do you like about writing?

What do you dislike about writing?

Have you ever had any good experiences as a writer?

Without referring to previous drafts, write a new description of your project (either a revision of the project you started with, or a new idea). (2 minutes)

How do you feel about writing as an exercise/practice as opposed to writing as an assignment on which you will be graded?

Rhetoric and persuading your community

In the previous section, I argued that a practice of writing can help you develop your own understanding of your research and your skill as a writer. That focuses on writing's impact on you, but writing is, of course, a tool of communication you use to engage your research community (including your professors) to get support for your work, and to get recognition for it, too.

Writing is more than just an expression of your ideas, it is an attempt to get them to make sense to a specific audience. A recognition of the audience is a crucial aspect of writing. To get a degree, to get published, and so on, your writings need to be accepted by the appropriate community or community representatives. If you're a graduate student writing a dissertation, you have to satisfy the reviewing professors. If you're seeking publication, you need to satisfy the editors and peer reviewers at journals or publishing houses. If you're seeking a fellowship or grant, you have to satisfy the appropriate boards. It's great to develop an important new idea through research, but it's much better to also be able to share the findings with others and to get credit for the work that you've done. Writing is how you get the credit.

Scholarly writing attempts to persuade the reader that the material presented is proper research, that the reasoning and evidence are sound, and that the conclusions are not just plausible but likely and indicated by the evidence. Persuasion is the art of rhetoric, and many writers use it effectively. One factor in being able to read other research literature effectively is to be able to recognize the use of rhetoric, and one factor in writing your own research literature effectively is to attend to your own work's need to persuade a specific audience.

Academic literature is filled with rhetorical devices to direct readers' attention away from gaps or problems in the argument and toward the strengths. Looking for the ways academic writing tries to persuade can help, both when trying to analyze and evaluate the reasoning used by others, and when developing your own written works.

Rhetoric—the art of persuasion—gets a bad rap. This can be seen in dictionary definitions, for example: "rhetoric: language designed to have a persuasive or impressive effect on its audience, but is often regarded as lacking in sincerity or meaningful content."[12] Students at most universities are taught "expository writing" which is defined in much less loaded terms: "intended to explain or describe something."[13] At most universities, rhetoric is taught only to those who seek it.

The basics of writing are often taught in isolation from rhetorical concerns, with writers attempting to limit themselves to "fact," without taking into account personal motivation, and often explicitly avoiding any use of the first person singular ("I").[14] Such writing can become a series of frustrating exercises in trying to follow the rules of composition and grammar while discussing subjects of minimal importance. This is not every student's experience, to be sure, but it is not uncommon.

The practice of separating writing from rhetoric helps create a situation in which new scholarly writers (i.e., graduate students) do not see the rhetorical dimension of their work, even though writing (or at least writing for publication) ultimately serves a rhetorical purpose.

One goal of this book is to help you, the scholarly writer, recognize the role of rhetoric in academic literature. By recognizing the rhetoric in the work of others, it becomes easier to see their theoretical weaknesses, giving you, perhaps, more confidence in the necessarily imperfect nature of your own work. Additionally, recognizing the rhetoric in the work of others may make it easier to use it yourself.

The proper and improper uses of rhetoric

The search for knowledge—philosophy—is what characterizes research and research institutions.[15] Rhetoric can be used to obscure knowledge, understanding, or truth. In this aspect, rhetoric is to be discouraged. But rhetoric can be used in service of understanding, too.

Many rhetorical devices can be used to distract the reader. For example, the well-known *ad hominem* argument links an abstract claim with a speaker whose veracity might be challenged, thus leading to a rejection of the claim without inspecting the claim itself (e.g., "Smith is a known liar, therefore Smith's claim XYZ must be rejected"). Or, for example, a speaker can dismiss a point as worthy of ridicule (e.g., "... Smith makes the laughable suggestion that XYZ, which can be rejected out of hand ..."), or assert its truth (e.g., "... the XYZ is obviously derived from ABC ..."). Such rhetorical techniques discourage critical challenges.

On the other hand, rhetorical devices can be used honestly to direct the reader's attention to desired issues. For example, by admitting a weakness, an author can often convince a reader that the author has been fundamentally responsible in carrying out research. If you say, "I am accepting premise X, even though I am aware that premise X is not universally accepted," you highlight a potential weakness in your work, but in so doing you also present yourself as fundamentally responsible in considering both the strengths and difficulties in your positions; it also suggests that you might have detailed information that you are not presenting.

Attempts to persuade are not inherently wrong.

Exercises (10 minutes)

How do you persuade an audience?

What do you need to know to persuade someone?

What parts of your own research are most difficult to persuade others to accept?

Cultivating confidence

Creating your own research requires confidence—the confidence to trust your own abilities as a researcher, and the confidence to pursue the lines of research that seem fruitful to you. If you are always following the guidance of another, then it's nearly impossible to do truly original work.

It is important to be able to follow the guidance of others, too, of course, but you need to keep these motivations in balance. In reading, you need both the confidence to challenge the ideas that others express, and the humility to challenge your own. In writing, you need the confidence to maintain your focus at the same time as you are humble enough to explicitly acknowledge the weaknesses in your work, especially those created by maintaining your focus.

Part of the purpose of this book is to help you cultivate confidence in your own work. I hope that by looking at literature from a rich perspective—one that can tease out the many different aspects of writing—you will have a better sense of options when writing. I also hope that by seeing research as a practice, you will recognize that this confidence, and the skills and knowledge that support it, will grow over time so long as you persevere in maintaining a regular research and writing practice.

Especially, I want to cultivate the recognition that every writer faces certain logical limits, so that writing is always negotiating the limits of certainty and always trying to negotiate the balance between confident assertion and tentative speculation. And that in the face of these limits, the writer is inevitably forced to use some sort of rhetorical device to limit the discussion—whether it is an explicit acknowledgment of a limitation or an implicit dismissal of some issue.

Exercises (15 minutes)

What are your strengths?

What are some abilities you would like to improve?

What steps can you take to improve those abilities?

Finishing your projects

There are many competing needs in life, and many corresponding purposes, and, speaking practically, your research has to fit within those practical boundaries. On the large scale, you need to think about how a project fits into your life. Suppose your focused pursuit of a method indicates a project that will take three years, do you follow that method? What if it looks like it will take five years? Personally, I believe that one of the great dangers of a "literature review" carried out near the beginning of a dissertation is the time that it takes. It's pretty easy to spend a term doing a literature review that doesn't move you any closer to designing your own project.

Always important to keep in mind, too, is how your own interests interact with the interests of others. Throughout this book, I emphasize the importance of turning inward and referring to your own judgment and having the confidence to criticize others. But it's also essential that you can criticize yourself and hear the criticism that is offered by others. To engage in the scholarly conversation effectively, you need confidence in your strong ideas, and the confidence, too, to admit the possibility that you're wrong or that you don't know.

A practice is made up of a series of efforts—projects large and small. While each specific project may rely on a specific method, the practitioner can experiment with using different methods.

Scholars face a series of projects. Starting as students, they produce works for class assignments, and then they progress to more independent research. Along the way, they have to describe their projects time and time again in different forums—from the informal description you share with friends, to any "elevator pitch" you develop to interest people who might help you, to coursework and seminar presentations, to administrative reports for your department, to applications for funding, not to mention any formal project proposal, and, of course, the final write-up you submit for review.

A crucial part of the practice of research is learning to put boundaries on projects so that you can complete them and share them with others in a timely fashion. An elevator pitch has to be short, but a dissertation? Who puts the limit on how long that takes? To a large extent, it's your choice whether to try to finish an imperfect, limited project or to keep pursing something better.

For you, as for other researchers, the questions of research never really end, even if you choose to stop pursuing answers. The imaginative scholar can always find new questions to ask.

Hopefully, you will finish individual projects, even if those projects are limited (as all projects are).

Central to the practice of research is writing up the research and sharing it with others as part of the communal research effort. Know your audience, know their expectations, and describe your work in a way that suits their expect-ations—which means keeping the schedules and producing work of the scope they expect. View it as a practice to develop your skill. Each new presentation is a trial for the next presentation. Don't get stuck on any one. Finish projects.

Exercises (10 to 20 minutes)

Do you have more problems starting projects or finishing them?

Do you have problems finishing projects?

What are some of the barriers that you face in finishing projects?

Project 2: the practice of research

What are the practical dimensions of your research?

Part 1: skills and abilities inventory
What skills do you have that are applicable to research?

Are there any specific skills for research that you want to develop or improve? (And, if there are none, that's no problem: this is for inventory, not for evaluation.)

Part 2: project planning
Describe the practical dimensions of your research project.

How long would it take to complete that project, from start to finish? (Make a rough estimate. Accuracy isn't crucial.)

How long would it take to complete that project in terms of hours of total effort expended (hours of work)?

What other resources would it take to complete the project?

Do you need special equipment?

Do you need to recruit participants?

Do you need to travel to some specific location?

Do you have access to these resources or can you get access to these resources?

How do you plan on allocating your effort and your resources?

Will your efforts be allocated equally across the whole duration of the project, or will there be periods where you do more and periods where you do less?

Notes

1 Of course, an experienced researcher who has already completed many studies probably also has a list of potential projects that has been growing for a long time, so they're not likely to be searching around for some new project.

2 Using the earlier cooking metaphor, we might say that the experienced chef will find it easier to adapt a recipe to new ingredients than would an inexperienced cook. An experienced chef missing one ingredient—the right kind of flour, perhaps—would be more likely to find a good substitute and make necessary changes to the recipe than an inexperienced cook.

3 Given the resources involved, I discourage graduate students from doing mixed-methods studies, especially if they are working on their first independent research project. If you are tempted to do a mixed-methods study for your dissertation, try planning successive phases of data collection, and writing your dissertation from the first phase alone.

4 I have no direct empirical evidence to support this, but I would be willing to bet that higher self-confidence correlates with higher dissertation completion rates.

5 At least not in terms of gathering new information. If you are reading more as part of a practice of improving your skill as a reader, then reading more does help.

6 Booth, Williams, and Colomb. 1995. University of Chicago Press.

7 There is a philosophical rabbit hole here that I do not want to explore: what is "thinking"? Understanding what "writing is thinking" means requires some idea of what "thinking" is, and that opens a vast theoretical debate about philosophy of mind/psychology/cognitive science.

8 Personally, I find a parallel between writing and teaching a class: in both contexts, statements and ideas that initially seem obvious can suddenly appear dubious. In a classroom, students often ask questions that I had not previously considered. In writing, reading what I have written often raises questions that I have not previously considered.

9 Here I recommend this practice from the perspective of how it influences your reasoning, but, as I discuss elsewhere, the practice will also

help with general writing skill, even if you're not worrying about grammar and the like.

10 To be sure, the beauty of Shakespeare's language explains part of the fame of Hamlet's soliloquy, but the emotional content—the idea—is what makes it stand out among all the beautiful words he wrote.

11 Writing beautifully may help a scholar, but it is not the standard by which scholarly work is primarily judged. Ethically speaking, you can hire an editor to fix your lousy prose, but you can't hire a researcher to fix your lousy research.

12 *New Oxford American Dictionary*, 2017.

13 *New Oxford American Dictionary*, 2017.

14 Avoiding the first person was common in the 20th century, but standards are changing on this, as evidenced, for example, by the popular college-writing book *They Say/I Say*, which gives a fundamental role to using the first person singular, as can be seen from the title. *They Say/I Say* does not focus on rhetoric or persuasion, but on shifting the idea of writing away from being "exposition" of a single idea to the idea of engaging in a conversation among many voices, a shift that forces the writer to consider their audience and how to reach their audience.

15 At least at their best. Obviously there are individuals and organizations who have falsified data or otherwise worked to mislead. But for this book, we are concerned with honest research.

One way to look at literature review is as a process of selecting material and reviewing (reading) that material. This loose definition covers a range of different activities: some literature reviews are very formal, using clearly defined criteria for selection/inclusion and methods of analysis to guide the whole process from start to finish.[1] Others are less formal and more flexible—a session browsing library shelves could be considered a literature review, or your whole career as a student could be considered a literature review preparing you to do your own research.

In the process of research design, while following the demands of the project, you might be called upon to do multiple different literature reviews: each time you make a commitment to some specific idea in your research project, you may benefit from doing a new literature review on that specific subject (providing resources are allocated reasonably). Such literature reviews may be informal, guided by your judgment as to when you have an answer that satisfies you, rather than by some fixed criteria. Because research design often involves surprises, formal reviews may be insufficient and inefficient, depending, as they do, on what you knew when you started the project, not on what you have learned since then.

Research and research design are difficult and fraught with uncertainty. You simply can't be certain what the best choices are. So where and how do you build a solid intellectual foundation for your research? You build that foundation on the publications of those scholars who have preceded you. In this way, you, like Newton, stand on the shoulders of the giants in your field.

Research design depends on your pursuit of your own individual project, but in that pursuit, the published literature in your field is a valuable tool: who has done work like the work you want to do? What did they do well? What did they do poorly? How can you learn from them to develop your own work? How do their stories about the world compare with yours? These are the questions that should guide reading to support research design.

For research design, the literature can be an invaluable tool to help you define a project that will be interesting to other members of your research community and help you develop your own voice to contribute to the scholarly discourse in your field. But the literature can also weigh you down if not used well.

The three chapters in this part of the book look at what goes into using literature effectively in the process of research design. The first chapter (Chapter 3) is concerned with attitudes and perspectives—most generally your own perspective in relationship to the readings: designing your own research requires confidence—either the confidence to build on and add to other people's work, or the confidence to critique it. More specifically, it discusses different perspectives and focuses to use when reading. The second and third chapters in the section turn toward more practical considerations. Chapter 4 is concerned with managing a wider body of literature, and general issues in dealing with all the things that you could read. Chapter 5 then concludes with reading, discussing specific issues for consideration when reading individual works, such as looking for models for your own work, and consideration of how other authors interact with the literature in their own writing.

Attitude

This whole book is built on the notion that approaching research differently will lead to interacting with the literature more effectively. Here the focus tightens on reading the literature, and the first concern is for your approach toward your research, which shapes your *attitude* as a reader.

I choose the word "attitude" here rather than, for example, "perspective," because the crucial shift that interests me is emotional: in the face of unavoidable uncertainty, it takes confidence to act. In my experience, people get lost in the literature for a combination of emotional and pragmatic reasons; not because they can't read well, but because their approach is off. People get overwhelmed with all that *could* be read; they feel that they don't know enough and haven't read enough; they feel, perhaps, awed and intimidated by the quality of the work they read. The problem isn't what they are able to do with the work, so much as what they choose to do with it. That's where attitude comes in.

As previously mentioned, reading effectively requires the confidence to challenge what you read, which depends on your view of yourself and your place in the community of researchers. If you want to do independent research (a dissertation, for example), how do you orient yourself to the literature and to the published authors who have created that literature (including, possibly, your own professors)? Must you accept everything you read or are told? If not, how do you decide what is valuable and what is not? Such questions require sufficient confidence to trust your own decisions.

Scholars need confidence. They need confidence to challenge ideas in the published literature, and thereby to find "gaps" in the literature that motivate new research. They need confidence in their own work to proceed even when their own work is uncertain or controversial.

Confidence ought not induce blindness to real critiques, of course. Confidence and doubt need to be kept in balance. Too much confidence leads to shoddy, careless work. Too much doubt leads to paralysis. With respect to using the literature effectively (and to research design more generally), the more common problem is lack of confidence, not lack of doubt. You have to have the confidence to enter into the conversation. This section focuses on developing the right attitude to use the literature to aid your research design.

Reasons to read scholarly literature for research design

"The purpose of reading is obvious," I imagine you saying. "The purpose of reading is to understand what the author has to say. It is to understand the theories and evidence presented." That's right, but it's too simple. For starters, it's difficult to understand theories and evidence, and it misses many dimensions of potential interest. But more significantly, it can miss possible nuance in your own purposes, as with, for example, the different purposes that motivate reading a work for the first time, and re-reading a work. The scholarly reader that returns to a work for a second reading has different purposes than the reader opening a work in a purely exploratory fashion.

The simple view of reading might be to "understand an author," but understanding is hardly simple. All writing—all language—is subject to differences in interpretation. Understanding what, precisely, a sentence or a word means, is not trivial. If interpretations were always clear and obvious, dictionaries would not have several definitions for many words; there would be no legal disputes on the meanings of contracts or laws; there would be no doctrinal debates about the meaning of foundational religious or spiritual texts. Scholarly literature is filled with different interpretations of the same words. How you understand a given word may well change over time as you read and explore.

In addition to the difficulties of interpretation, all writing invites the question of whether the author was successful in conveying his or her ideas. In my own experience, the words I write are not always understood as I would wish. There have been times I tried to say "X" and my reader thought I was saying "Y." This often happens when I am revising my work: I often see a sentence I have written that doesn't convey what I want. Writing is hard. Expressing complex ideas in words is hard. Sometimes authors fail in their aim, and the words on the page don't capture the author's reasoning. Given how many works are edited and revised after publication, it would seem that published authors (or their publishers) often feel a desire to rewrite their own works.

If a work is difficult to understand, it might be due to the writer's limitations as a writer, not your lack of intelligence.[2]

Further, academic writing wants to engage with the complexity of the observed world. Despite its reputation for being out of touch, academic writing tries to describe the real world, and the observed world typically reveals important detailed complexity when closely examined. The complexity of the task of research itself permeates academic writing, and it plays out in the many different levels at which academic literature operates.[3] So, yes, the purpose of reading is to understand what the writer is saying. But that is not a simple thing. Part of developing your own scholarly voice is to develop your own interpretations of other people's work.

In addition to the main ideas of a work, the reader of academic literature can also learn a lot about the larger research community in which an author works. A published piece of scholarly writing will place itself in the context of other research in the field by citing works of the people with whom they agree and disagree, thus giving a sense of how the authors view their communities. The literature also expresses ideas about research methods and research theory and about the conventions of communication in your field.

I don't imagine that any of these concerns are surprising. But putting them into practice can be difficult. I believe that being consciously aware of these different factors can ultimately help you read more effectively—not with less effort, but with greater return for the effort invested.

Practice and the student driver analogy

Trying to manage all the many different issues in scholarly works can be overwhelming, especially when the central theoretical component is itself hard to understand. Adding other tasks—evaluating the quality of the work, seeing the context in which the work is set, examining the method, etc.—increases the difficulty of an already difficult task. But the complexity is, I think, more intimidating than difficult. Yes, you do have to manage many different things, but with practice they become a natural part of your process.

A useful analogy, I think, is learning to drive a car.

Driving a car is basically simple: you press the gas and use the steering wheel to direct the car where you want to go. A child could do it.

The actual experience of driving, however, and doing it well, has many complications—other motorists, pedestrians, traffic lights, road signs, turn signals, side and rear-view mirrors, etc.—that make learning to drive somewhat less than simple. When you first drive, it can feel a little overwhelming to attend to all these different things at once. But the more time spent behind the wheel, the easier it is to integrate all the different aspects into one smooth operation. With enough practice, all these little issues become a natural part of the process and you can give all your attention to simply going where you want to go.[4]

With reading scholarly literature, the main purpose—where you want to go—is to understand how a specific work relates to your own research, and, as noted, that relationship can manifest in many important ways. With practice, these different issues that seem to demand separate attention become more easily integrated into one coherent process centered on defining your own research project as part of a larger scholarly conversation.

Exercises (5 to 30 minutes)

Why do you read? What do you hope to get from reading? Consider as many different dimensions of motivation and expectation as you can. For example, you might read to satisfy your professors and also to satisfy your own curiosity in a general sense, and/or to answer some very specific question.

How do you feel when reading? Overwhelmed or in charge? Confident or doubtful?

Reasons to read 2: personal purpose

You will have different purposes for reading at different times, and those different purposes impact how you read the material. In the previous section, I discussed the basic difference between reading something for the first time and re-reading something, but that basic difference itself hides a bunch of nuance in your own purposes. Every time you read a work, your purposes may shift, depending on your situation.

There are two general types of reading that I'll discuss: exploratory and instrumental.

Sometimes you read to explore—to consider completely new ideas, to see new perspectives. Even if you are keeping your focus on the same topic, there are usually a range of different ideas. For example, in the study of psychotherapy, psychodynamic and cognitive behavioral are only two among a wide array of different theories. In cognitive science, there are computational theories of thought (mind as computer), and there are biological theories of thought (embodied mind). In economics and political science, there are theories of humans as rational decision-makers, and there are theories of humans as irrational decision-makers. There is value in exploring such variety.

In exploratory reading, you are open to new ideas, and looking for new ideas. This is a great approach when you're doing coursework and just beginning to think about your own project. But when it's time to commit to a project, exploratory reading can be detrimental.

When it's time to design your own project, it's necessary to stop exploring and start committing to aspects of your own research project. If you're trying to research psychodynamic therapy, time spent reading about cognitive behavioral theories doesn't move your own work forward.[5]

The more you have committed to the definition of a project, the more focused your reading can be on developing your own project. Such reading is "instrumental" in that it serves a specific purpose. For example, you can read looking for models for your own research—while this still has an exploratory dimension, it has a more focused purpose: it's not just reading to learn new theories, it's reading with the specific purpose of finding individual projects that you can model for your own research. Or, for example, before committing to a project, you might read a book on research methods in an exploratory fashion, wondering which methods to use; then, once you make a commitment to a project, you go back to that book for detailed guidance about your chosen method.

As you commit to a project, you can read asking, "how does this help my project?" You read looking for sources you can use to structure your project. This kind of reading helps focus on specific definitions to use for each of your main concepts, or helps you refine your choice of methods, or helps you define the question that you are addressing.

Reading, therefore, is not always the same thing. Try to recognize the different purposes you have for reading a given work: how will it help you? Is it exploratory? Is it going to help you with some specific aspect of your project? Read with a suitable purpose.

Exercises (10 minutes)

What are some of the different purposes to read? What are general purposes? What about more situation-specific purposes?

How to read: your attitude

What does it mean to be an independent scholar? What does it mean to do original research? Whatever else these might mean, at heart these questions speak to the need for the scholar—you—to make your own decisions. You need to take charge of your research; you cannot simply let others tell you what to do.[6] To use research literature effectively, you need to believe in yourself enough to challenge others.

If your overall task as a researcher is to design a research project that will help tell a coherent story about the world, and you're reading literature to help make your own story richer and more detailed so that you can design a better project, then you want to make sure you only use the best of the different ideas you read. If you read accepting everything, if you assume that all published work is correct and that you must accept it, then you'll never develop your own independent views of the world. If you accept each new piece as equally valuable, then you end up drowning in a sea of disparate ideas. You must believe that your own vision of the world is valuable, and that your own ideas and work as a scholar (refined by diligent use of methods, reasoning, and the standards of your research community, of course) can make a worthy contribution to your field.

Scholarship generally grows out of the basic sense that current theory is lacking in some way—maybe a subject that has not been covered, or an error in current theory. Such "gaps" in the literature can be found by reading with a challenging and questioning attitude—often quite simply. They're easy to miss if you're too deferential and assume that the authors are much smarter than you. For many graduate students, challenging the literature does not come naturally, especially with habits built from previous schooling.

In elementary school through secondary school and much of college, and even into some graduate studies, you're expected to follow and repeat what the teacher tells you. But if you're writing a doctoral dissertation or master's thesis, or writing for publication, you are expected to do original work, and it isn't enough to just repeat what others say. You must read believing you have both the right and the ability to do research that adds to the scholarly conversation. This means, generally, that you must read with evaluative intent: which research is good? Which is weak? An element of doubt is crucial: scholars do not accept the accepted wisdom; they test it.

Additionally, reading must be done with respect to your attempt to define and refine your own views of the world, which form the foundation for your research project. Which ideas fit with your own, and which don't? Be open to ideas that disagree with yours and willing to learn that you may be wrong, but also be confident enough to reject those ideas if you have good reasons. Sometimes, you will find work that is of high quality but that doesn't fit your own ideas; other times you may agree with a work in spite of obvious flaws. Such differences between what you think and what you read can provide avenues for research.

You need to develop your own theories, which means choosing a set of specific voices with whom you will have a conversation—both the voices that you want to echo and the voices you want to correct or contradict.

Where do you allocate your resources?

There is a vast body of published literature and it can be easy to slip into the trap of thinking that you have not yet read enough. You'll never read everything. And if "enough" means having no more questions, you'll never read enough. As previously mentioned, you have limited resources—limited time, limited energy, limited interest—and you need to use those resources effectively. There will always be more reading that you *could* do. If you think that you *should* do every task that you *could* do, then you'll always feel the burden of not having done enough. Where will you allocate your resources?

There is a lot to read (and to write about). How will you deal with the demands on your time? You can approach each work with deep intensity, striving to understand it intimately, or you can approach each work quickly, skimming for main points and trying to understand the larger discourse. The first allows deeper knowledge of a smaller number of works, while the second allows wider knowledge of the published literature. These two approaches might reflect deeper attitudes: the perfectionist might tend to the first approach (and get stuck trying to be perfect), while the "get-it-done" pragmatist might tend to the second (and miss important details). Practically speaking, it is best to maintain something of a balance between the two.

Given limited time, you are forced to make a choice between 1) reading something new, 2) re-reading something for a deeper understanding, or 3) doing something else—like writing about and developing your own work. If you spend too much time on the reading, you never get to other necessary parts of conducting research, which means never finishing any project.

As part of your research practice, you get to choose where to spend your attention and effort. How do you divide your resources between reading and other tasks? And how you allocate the time that you do have for reading? Make sure to allocate time for writing about your own project, no matter how much you want to read.

Exercises (15 minutes)

What is the difference between an independent researcher and a student? Do you identify as a student or an independent researcher? Why? If you view yourself as an independent scholar, why? What characteristics do you have that qualify you as such? If you do not view yourself as an independent scholar, what stands between you and that status? What needs to change?

Heroes and villains

When reading fiction, it's natural to agree with some characters and disagree with others, and to like some characters and dislike others. These responses to characters help us identify the "heroes" and "villains" in the works we read. Sometimes it's easy: Beowulf is a hero and Grendel is a villain; Dorothy is a hero and the Wicked Witch is a villain.[7] And sometimes it's not so easy: is Hamlet a hero?

To some extent, we can find heroes and villains in academic writing as well. Because this is a section on attitude, which is at least partly emotional, I choose the terms "hero" and "villain" to amplify the emotional stakes. With fiction, most people feel every right to their emotional responses. But with academic writing, most people learn to read in contexts that call for understanding and satisfying the interests of a professor, rather than identifying personal responses. These contexts often presume academic writing's claim to authority (and often to objectivity), which can intimidate readers from making their own judgments. To use academic writing most effectively, it's necessary to make decisions that separate heroes (people and ideas you agree with) from villains (those you don't).

Citing heroes and villains helps people see where you stand. As the written manifestation of the conversation between scholars, academic writing relies on explicit comparisons with other works (which represent the other voices with whom an author is conversing)—that's one reason the practice of citation is so important. Generally, people talk about citation in terms of giving credit where credit is due, but citation is also an aid to explanation: by citing a specific author, you invoke a whole set of ideas that will be familiar to your readers. If your readers know the source you cite, they can better understand your work.

As mentioned earlier, Immanuel Kant famously wrote that he was "woken from dogmatic slumbers" by Hume. Motivated by a sense of Hume's errors, Kant developed his *Prolegomena to Any Future Metaphysics*, one of his most significant and influential works. Hume provides the background against which Kant developed his corrective ideas.[8] In the emotionally amplified language of this section, Hume is the villain in Kant's work.

The comparison of accepted explanations with rejected explanations is at the heart of learning. Much of learning consists in replacing old ideas with new ones. The idea that Santa Claus brings Christmas presents is replaced with the idea that parents have bought them. The idea of Newtonian physics is replaced with Einstein's general relativity. Hume's ideas about knowledge are replaced with Kant's or with Popper's, or those of some other scholar.

At times, the theoretical debates are so heated that it is no exaggeration to speak of people finding actual heroes or villains. Galileo, of course, was jailed and excommunicated. Karl Marx was a hero to many and to others a villain. As was Sigmund Freud. The emotional stakes are not so high in all debates, but for many, scholarship is truly filled with heroes and villains.

To the extent that academic writing gives a starring role to ideas, the ideas are the heroes or villains. But the scholars who express an idea become avatars of the idea, and thus the potential "hero" or "villain" of some scholarly work that opposes it (as, for example, Popper did with Hume and the problem of induction).

Identifying the heroes and villains in your reading, and explicitly identifying specific ideas that you accept or reject, will help you develop a better sense of the larger body of literature in your field. This is a useful way to look at the community of scholars and the variety of ideas that have been expressed in the published literature.[9]

When you read, look for your own heroes or villains: with what or whom do you agree or disagree? And also look for the heroes and villains of the author: with what or whom is the author agreeing or disagreeing?

Foundations rather than heroes

Scholarly works are built on ideas, and those ideas come from somewhere. Some ideas are original, but typically people start with beliefs that they share with (and have learned from) others. Marxist economists work within one structure of beliefs (in which Marx is a hero). Free Market economists work in another (with Adam Smith as hero).

It is not uncommon to see academic works discussing "theoretical foundations" or "conceptual frameworks." These foundations and frameworks are ideas that the author accepts, which, in the literature, often appear as discussions of specific authors.

As a writer, it is important to explicitly identify the specific ideas and theories that shape a particular work, and as a scholar, it is good to be able to consciously identify the ideas that shape your reasoning. Identifying heroes can help in this process. If you find yourself agreeing with something you read, identifying the author as a hero is a good first step. The next step is to identify the specific ideas that you want to retain. Knowing your heroes can help focus your reading, because it's important to read the work of the scholars with whom you most closely align. If we are thinking of scholarship as a conversation, it is the closely aligned scholars with whom it is most important to interact. Yes, there are times when a Marxist economist and a Free Market economist might have a conversation, but it's hard to move research forward if you never commit to any foundational principles—principles that you accept without debate (in the context of a given project, at least). If two Marxists work together, they don't have to debate basic principles, and they can focus their attention on some more detailed project that furthers Marxist discourse. Knowing your heroes gives you an opportunity to build a theoretical foundation for your work.[10]

Foils rather than villains

In practical terms, it is probably better to think of the "villains" as foils to be used in defining your own work. You can use other scholars to provide contrasts that help reveal important characteristics of something under examination.

For this reason, it can be useful to choose highly respected authors as your "villains." The more famous your foil, the more likely that your audience will understand the work that is the basis of the comparison. The better the quality of the work, the less the chance that you will be arguing against a straw man (an argument that is too weak to be taken seriously).

For example, I have used Herbert Simon as a foil. Simon is a Nobel Prize-winning psychologist and economist, renowned for his work on decision-making, design, and artificial intelligence. When my mentor (Jean-Pierre Protzen) and I were writing about his mentor, Horst Rittel,[11] it was natural to use Simon as a foil because of their disagreement on a fundamental point of design theory: Rittel believed that no definitive formulation of a design problem was possible under any circumstances,[12] while Simon believed that a rational definition was logically possible and that only practical limitations stood in the way of such a definition. Simon is a good foil because of his fame and the quality of his work: his fame means that readers in design theory will know his work, allowing reference to a whole set of ideas without a lengthy discussion of those ideas. Because his work is of high quality, it provides a valuable contrast readers can respect—he's no straw man.

Hero and villain in one person

For a scholar, it can be extremely useful to find a figure who is simultaneously hero and villain, in the sense that they provide many useful foundational ideas, and also provide at least one valuable idea that can be used as a contrast—either an error to correct or an absence to address. If you can find such a figure, you can often build a research project effectively by leaning heavily on their work—you adopt their overall framework at the same time as focusing on one specific limitation in their work.

Who are the author's heroes and villains?

I have been suggesting that in reading you want to identify your own heroes and villains, but it's also useful to identify the heroes and villains of the author whose work you're currently reading. Recognizing the relationships between scholars gives you a sense of the community in which they operate, and seeing how other scholars engage with their heroes and villains will help you build your own research and research writing more effectively.

To emphasize the emotional aspect of attitude, I spoke of heroes and villains. While the scholar should be striving for a clear framing of ideas that allows them to enter into the scholarly discourse and be understood,[13] the emotional dimension—the confidence to critique and/or support—is superior to trying to maintain a permanent neutrality based on a simplistic idea of research objectivity, or on the assumption that you are not competent or capable of challenging published authors. Unless you believe in yourself sufficiently to challenge the work of prior scholars, it is very difficult to use other literature effectively in producing your own research.

Exercises (1 minute, repeat 10 to 30 times)

Identify a hero or villain. Cite a work by that person (from memory, don't go searching reference lists).

Why is so much academic writing bad?

Academic writing has a well-deserved reputation as being difficult and inelegant. Poor writing is sometimes accepted in academia because what is most important is conceptual content, and if a poorly written work has strong conceptual content, it may become important in the discourse.

In your approach to academic literature, I suggest a certain sympathy for bad writing, based on the idea that it may result from the attempt to discuss novel concepts. Granted, it is difficult to read poor writing. But could the ideas be a model for your own work? To what extent was the author struggling to express him or herself (if you struggle to write, can you imagine the other author also struggling)? What is it about the subject matter that led the author to this presentation of ideas? And what did others see in the work when they read it?

Academic writing can be bad, and many important ideas are presented in difficult writing. You can despise the writing of, for example, a Judith Butler or a Jacques Derrida (who are known for difficult prose), but in certain research communities you're going to be crippled if you can't discuss their ideas in a cogent fashion. Although I have been promoting being a critical reader, on this point I argue for the opposite: set aside complaints about the quality of the writing and focus on the structure of the reasoning.[14] Recognize the difficulties in writing well: many scholars struggle to write clearly about difficult-to-explain concepts.

It is my hope that recognizing these difficulties and seeing a relationship between the bad writing that you read and your own struggles in writing will help you approach the literature more effectively as both reader and writer, or at least with greater equanimity.

Academic writing is primarily judged with respect to the underlying ideas and reasoning, and therefore poor writing about good ideas can survive and prosper on the basis of its underlying intellectual strength. This will be true for your own writing, too: if your underlying ideas are well defined and developed, then your work is more likely to be accepted. While you should strive to write well, your focus should be on the concepts you're discussing, not on trying to create beautiful prose. It's hard enough to write about a developing research project without worrying whether your text is elegant enough.[15]

Academic writing and legal writing

In a way, scholarly writing is much like legal writing, which also has a reputation for being poorly written and hard to read and understand. Legal writing—"legalese"—is quite reasonably known for complexity and obscurity, but that complexity is an unavoidable result of its purpose, just as the complexity of scholarly writing is a result of the purpose of academic writing.[16] Both legal writing and academic writing share a desire to be as clear as possible and to eliminate ambiguity and uncertainty in interpretation, which contributes to very careful phrasing and complex language. Legal and scholarly writing both attempt to take all possibilities into account. Thus a contract governing a simple transaction—the purchase of an item, for example—will contain many clauses, each addressing a different possible outcome or aspect of the transaction—what happens if the item fails (and what about different kinds of failure)? Who takes responsibility? Who is liable? Does the purchaser have any commitments —for example, are there any restrictions on whether the purchaser is allowed to sell the item?

Similarly, scholarly literature tries to take different possibilities into account, seeking alternative explanations and limits of various claims. All these concerns contribute to complexity and obscurity, despite the best intentions for clarity and definition. As with legal writing, it is desirable to take into account as many conditions or caveats as possible. Thus a scholar who has collected data is expected to discuss possible reasons that the data collection was biased or otherwise limited, as well as reasons that the analytical method might be limited, and then must also take into account any other concerns that limit the generalizability of the conclusions drawn from the analysis. This creates a situation where a large proportion of the writing is not directly concerned with the main point of the work, but rather with talking about the limits of the work. It is similar to many contracts (e.g., terms of service on a website) where there may be one or two clauses representing the basic principle (what services are provided), several clauses defining terms, and then a long list of clauses that detail specific conditions, responsibilities, or limitations (to liability, to what services will be provided, to what guarantees will be made, etc.). For the scholar, like the lawyer, attention to detail is crucial, and attention to detail can lead to long and difficult written works.

Complexity of material and complexity of language: an apology for jargon

One reason that academic writing can be difficult to read is the use of jargon—specialized language that is obscure to non-specialists.

Jargon arises from the desire to speak about subjects that are outside the everyday subjects for which most language is used. Heavy use of jargon can make reading very difficult. But if the work requires specificity and attention to issues that are not common, then everyday language may not suit.

Jargon arises from a need. If there is a need to make distinctions between two things commonly grouped together, words will arise to describe the distinction, and the resulting language may seem impenetrable to someone who is unfamiliar with the discourse.

Jargon is stereotyped as bad language, but it is an indispensable tool when used well. Jargon is often overused and it would be great if all academics using jargon could also translate those concepts into regular language for an everyday audience, but the ability to describe specialized work in accessible terms is not a requirement for a scholar.[17] Scholarly work is judged by experts—professors or peer reviewers—not boards of random laypeople.

If you're having trouble reading something because of extensive use of jargon, consider reading other works in the same area. Try to get a sense of how other authors talk about the same set of issues. Some authors will create unnecessary jargon, but much jargon is shared by the members of the community, so if you're having trouble with the language of one author, you might have success with a different author, which would then give you guidance for understanding the first, more difficult work. This point again suggests the value in reading widely and not struggling excessively through a single work (emphasis on the word "excessively"—some works will only yield with a struggle, but they're worth the effort; other works are better put aside—for later or for never).

Exercises (10 minutes, repeat a few times)

Think of an example of a work that is difficult to read but well written, or a work that is difficult to read and poorly written. What is it about the writing that is difficult? Long sentences? Big words? Grammatical errors? If the work is a good work, why does it transcend the difficulty of its language?

Different definitions, different ideas

In scholarly writing, precision and attention to detail are expected. And since research is striving to explore the unknown and undefined, specialized language (jargon) can arise. When jargon manifests as novel words, we can recognize it easily and we can deal with it or ignore it as we wish. But this need to discuss novel ideas can also appear in another difficult form in the research literature: a single word, even a fairly common one, can and will be used in many different ways, and scholars will often care greatly about these differences.

Looking in any large dictionary will reveal multiple listed definitions for many words.[18] Words are difficult to define, even when simply trying to define conventional usage, which may often include several distinct meanings. This becomes a matter of import and difficulty in academic writing.

One of the better known examples of such a novel use is Thomas Kuhn's use of the word "paradigm" in his famous *Structure of Scientific Revolutions*. Prior to Kuhn's work, "paradigm" generally meant "model" and was mostly used in the discussion of rhetoric. Kuhn's work, however, led to debates on what can be considered a "paradigm," or at least debates on what can be considered a "scientific paradigm."

An example of this issue that I remember from my studies in design theory comes from the beginning of J. C. Jones's book *Design Methods: Seeds of Human Futures*, which opens its first chapter with a list of some eleven different definitions of design. As a student in a program in "design theories and methods in architecture," I had to have some idea of what *I* thought design was, and seeing all the different definitions did not simplify that.

Different definitions focus attention differently. To follow the example of defining *design*, we might first note that the word is both noun and verb—there are "designs" and there are people who "design" objects—and this, in itself, is an issue that must be considered in order to focus research. Looking at *design* as a noun directs your attention to objects; *design* as a verb focuses attention on activities. If you focus on *design*, the verb—the process of designing—then your definition will determine which activities you study. Is an architect designing when drawing up plans? Is a sculptor designing when working in the studio? Is a researcher designing when planning a research project? Which activities count as design?

Choice of definition will focus attention, and will also align you with (or in opposition to) the work of other scholars. When you read other scholars' work, look for their definitions and how they are used to manage the scope of the work and to limit the extent of the research. Consider the practical dimensions of the definition chosen: how does the definition shape the rest of the material considered? How would the work be different if they chose a different definition?

In designing your own research, don't get stuck vacillating between definitions: make a commitment to one definition until you finish a project.[19] If you see many different definitions when reading the literature, it's important to consider what you like and dislike about each. It's not unlikely that you'll find different strengths and weaknesses, which can make it hard to choose between definitions. But if you don't commit to one definition, you can end up spending your time debating the variety of definitions rather than designing your own project.

While it's useful to know the different definitions used by important scholars, it may be more useful to look at them as variations on an attempt to define an elusive concept that you yourself may need to define in your own research. The differences between definitions arise from different ideas of what is important. What is important to you? Which definitions suit those concerns? If a definition doesn't suit you, why? When it's time to write, it will be important to be able to explain the definitions that you use.

In line with the general concern of this section, approach the material with the right attitude: other people's definitions are interesting for what they can tell you about your own work. Other people's definitions may be useful supports on which to build your work, but no-one else's definition is a strict limit on your work. You need a definition that you can stick with for a whole project—for *your* project. Commit to a definition that works for you and that allows you to set limits that make your project more practical. Therefore, when reading, it is crucial to look at different definitions critically with an eye to their strengths and weaknesses, both as abstract concepts and as guides to your own research projects.

Exercises (10 minutes, repeat two or three times)

Choose a word that is crucial to your work but is hard to define. Try to define it without referring to any works. Check its dictionary definition. Do you know any works that use the term and provide a definition for it? List other definitions. Do these definitions agree?

Remember: this is an exercise! Don't overwork it. Engage the ideas. Get some practice. Keep it in balance.

Breaking down arguments

The world is complex (i.e., it has many interconnected parts), and so theories about the world and the research done to develop and test those theories are complex. Therefore, it is useful to be able to manage complexity by separating out different ideas that are working together in the literature you read. The complex arguments found in published literature link many different issues and concerns. Often, some parts of an argument are extremely valuable while others are not.

In the discussion of practical concerns that follows, I separate out different aspects of a larger project for consideration—the main point, the motivation, the claims of significance, the methods, the audience, rhetorical structures, and more—but here I am focused on the willingness to break apart the different aspects of an argument—the various assumptions made, the conclusions drawn from those assumptions, the definitions used, the choices of method and focus, and other such concerns. It is valuable to be able to use the parts that help you and not the rest.

Breaking down complex arguments can often be useful, especially if you want to use ideas expressed by controversial authors.

Many important ideas come into public recognition as part of a larger conceptual structure that is problematic. One famous example of this is the development of psychodynamic theories. Generally, psychodynamic theories are associated with Freud (who, of course, did not himself work in a vacuum), but Freudian theories are famously loaded with many highly controversial ideas—for example, the notion of penis envy. Psychodynamic scholars following Freud's main ideas have often adopted much of the theory of how the mind operates while rejecting some of the problematic assumptions. Being able to break apart the different parts of Freud's arguments allows use of his best ideas without the burden of his worst.

Speaking generally, when you're dealing with complex ideas, there is a richness that can be analyzed, by which I mean broken into parts (true to the etymology of "analysis," the converse of "synthesis" or the putting of parts together into a whole). If you are able to distinguish and separate the different ideas that are working together in an argument, it becomes easier to pick pieces that help you while setting aside ones that will interfere.

It's a good skill to practice because it can help you refine your own theories: as with the theories of other authors, you can keep the good pieces and separate out pieces you would like to revise.

Exercises (10 to 15 minutes)

Perhaps the easiest way to see complexity in an idea is to review something familiar—a restaurant, movie, etc.—do you like or dislike it? What do you like or dislike? Make a list of pros and cons. Pick some specific pros and cons, and consider whether they are complex. If, for example, you review a restaurant, and one reason you like it is they have your favorite dish, what is good about that dish? Is it your favorite everywhere or just at the restaurant? Or, if reviewing a movie, perhaps you liked visual effects—what were the different effects that you liked? What did you like about them? Were there any aspects that you didn't like?

Consider one specific idea from one specific author. Consider its implications. Consider how it relates to other ideas that you use. What assumptions/presuppositions does it rely on? What are objections to the idea that you have seen expressed by other writers (if any)? Do you have any objections or concerns about the idea?

Finding the sources for your own ideas

Scholars are supposed to do original work. But originality doesn't mean overturning all previous knowledge. Darwin was original, but he was not the first to posit evolution. Einstein was original, but he shared many assumptions with others. Newton saw farther, but as he said, he was standing on the shoulders of giants (i.e., using their ideas). We may have many completely original ideas, but we still share many ideas with others, too: the sharing is necessary to participate in communities, and it's a natural outcome of that participation.

Earlier, I discussed the importance of using what you already know and making your own ideas explicit. An important step in making ideas explicit is examining their sources. Which are completely your own, and which have you learned from others? And of the ideas that you have learned from others, from whom have you learned them, and where?

It's likely that you have ideas that you use and you consciously know the source of the idea from some specific reading of your own. For example, you might be familiar with the work of Thomas Kuhn, the famous scientific historian mentioned earlier, who developed the idea of "scientific revolutions" and "scientific paradigms." Or you might associate Freud with ideas like the id and the ego. In such cases, you explicitly know sources (even if you don't know those sources very well!).

There might be other ideas that you have learned consciously, perhaps from professors or fellow students, but whose direct source you don't know. For example, you might have heard of "scientific paradigms" and "scientific revolutions" from some professor or friend; you might even have discussed the ideas without knowing about Thomas Kuhn. In such cases, at least you have some idea of the source of the idea as external, and can begin the process of tracking it down.

Additionally, you probably also have ideas that you learned relatively early and internalized and couldn't trace to a source. Ideas like the operation of reward and punishment in educational processes or the law of supply and demand are ideas that are so common in our culture that it would be easy to learn them at a relatively young age from a variety of sources, both in and out of educational settings (e.g., a character in a screen drama about schools might talk about reward and punishment; a character in a screen drama about business might talk about supply and demand).[20]

As a first step for getting familiar with the ideas that you do use, sort out the ones for which you can identify a source. And then seek out the sources that you can identify, both immediately (e.g., "My professor mentioned this in lecture") and historically ("The idea my professor expressed was taken from the work of Einstein [or whomever]").

For the ideas for which you can't identify a source, the situation will dictate whether you need to find a good source or not. The more heavily you rely on any particular idea, the greater your need to find its sources.

In the abstract, you may not need a source for an idea: you can rely on, for example, the idea of inquiry-based education in setting up a study without needing to cite any other source. But to share that work with a community, and to make it meaningful for that community, your ability to cite sources helps explain your ideas to others and helps them see that you are not simply replicating previous work.[21]

Therefore, when you read, you want to keep an eye out to see if you can identify sources for what you already believe: if you read something that puts forth an idea with which you agree, you can ask yourself whether to use the work as a source of that idea. Would you cite this work for the idea? If not, who/what would you cite? Does the author cite any sources on that idea?

When you read, keep an eye out for authors who express ideas with which you agree: such expressions can become citations you use to back up your own arguments. This allows the jump from recognizing your own thinking, to identifying sources for those ideas, to being able to explain to others how your own research relates to sources in the literature.

Being able to recognize your own ideas as a theory and to compare your theory to the work of other scholars is a crucial step in a research practice.

Distinguishing "common knowledge" from ideas needing citation

One challenge that the academic writer faces is deciding whether or not an idea needs citation. Some claims are so widely known or accepted, they don't need citation. You don't have to cite Copernicus to claim the earth orbits the sun. When writing, it can be difficult to judge whether a claim is common knowledge or whether it needs a specific citation. The roots of handling this elegantly lie in being able to recognize the community norms.

To some extent, you can learn these norms by observing how other authors handle citation: when do they use citation and when do they leave it out? Ideas can be introduced as implicitly acceptable, as needing support but not citation, or as needing citation, and some authors will be more careful about citing ideas than others. Seeing how other writers handle this kind of issue allows you to develop a sense of how to handle the same issues yourself.

Of course, you will learn more by submitting a draft to someone who will critique it. Most specifically, if you're concerned with which ideas will need citation in your work, you can submit a draft, and see what citations your reader(s) demand.

Read as if you were a professor reading the work of a student

This is the last section of the discussion of attitude, so I'm going to close with what might be a simple suggestion, one that many graduate students have practical experience with: read like a teacher. Think about how you read the work of students and how professors have read your work. What do you look for in a student's work? Can you not look for the same things in a published article? There is no question that a published work is of higher quality than a class assignment, but published works are hardly perfect. You can read the works of other scholars with the same critical eye a teacher turns on a student. When the authors introduce a new idea, do they cite a source? Which ideas do they cite, and which do they accept as given? Are those choices justified? And how do their choices of idea and source help you? Is it good enough that you would want to work with this person, that you would judge them a competent scholar? Are grammar and style good?[22] Even if you're reading the work of a Nobel Prize-winner, read as if you have the right and responsibility to judge the quality of the work. To be an independent researcher, you have to be willing to challenge other published scholars—they are the voices to which you respond. Even when reading, you need the confidence to express your own voice. For one good research project, you don't need to be brilliant; you just need to find one good idea for a project in response to something you have read.

> **Exercises** (1 minute. Repeat 15 to 20 times.)
>
> Write down an idea that you would like to use in your work. Where did you get that idea? Have you ever heard that idea from someone else? From whom?

Project 3: being critical

In my experience, even though many students suffer from lack of confidence when thinking about their own work, in the right contexts, they are confident enough to criticize at least some of what they read. For many, there are times they are confident enough to say, "the author is off the wall," but that confidence dissolves into, "I have no idea what I'm trying to say," when it's time to write. In a conversation with a fellow student, it's easy to deliver and feel confident about a loose, off-the-cuff critique of someone else's work. But when it's time to write that down and present it to professors, doubt creeps in, as well as social pressure to be polite and show respect for published authors. You need to feel the power to critique. You want to be judicious, of course, but you need to practice being critical, too.

When writing, many turn their critical eye on themselves, and struggle to write or make progress because of the intense criticism they direct at themselves. Some self-criticism is necessary, but it needs to be balanced with a willingness to critique other work as well. This project is an exercise in turning the critical eye outward.

1   Identify one piece of published research that you think is weak—the worst piece that you have read, if you can think of such a thing.

What is bad about it? Describe its strengths and weaknesses, in detail, if possible. Is it poorly written? Is the reasoning unclear or incoherent? Is the method poorly developed? What about it makes you critical?

To what extent is your dislike of the work based on theoretical differences?

To what extent is your dislike of the work based on stylistic or rhetorical concerns?

Offer constructive criticism for improving that work.

2   Identify one piece of work that you would like to build upon.

What is good about it? Describe its strengths and weaknesses, in detail, if possible. Is it poorly written? Is the reasoning unclear or incoherent? Is the method poorly developed? What about it makes you critical?

To what extent is your like for the work based on theoretical agreements?

To what extent is your like for the work based on stylistic or rhetorical concerns?

Offer constructive criticism for improving that work.

Notes

1   Or at least most of the process. As noted earlier, researchers cannot rely on methods for choice of subject or method.

2   Again, read with confidence! Assume that you have the right, the knowledge, the ability, and the responsibility to evaluate the work.

3   One invaluable skill for a researcher is to be able to recognize the complexity in apparently simple matters—to see, for example, the range of possible meanings or implications that might be attributed to one sentence. Another invaluable skill is to be able to manage this complexity by making reasonable compromises to avoid drowning in a sea of complicating detail.

4   Indeed, many drivers find they don't even need all their attention to get to where they're going, allowing concentration on other matters as well.

5   Of course, if you wanted to somehow integrate psychodynamic and cognitive behavioral therapies, then you would need to read in both areas. The point here is that there comes a time to stop exploratory reading.

6   Obviously, there are times where it is necessary to satisfy a professor or reviewer. But such situations do not eliminate the independence of the researcher.

7   Actually, I chose these two examples because more recent novels—John Gardner's *Grendel* and Gregory Maguire's *Wicked*—have re-presented these villains in much more sympathetic forms.

8   This is an example of how scholarship is a manifestation of an exchange of ideas—a conversation—between scholars.

9   Appropriate in developing your research practice, at least. As a writer, it's usually prudent to avoid labeling your interlocutors as real villains, but rather to focus on specific premises they use. As I say above, my choice of terms amplifies the emotional content, which isn't always beneficial.

10 In the abstract, scholarly independence means a willingness to overturn any and all ideas. That's great. Practically speaking, however, on almost any point, there will be people with whom you agree and disagree. You can cooperate with the people you agree with or debate with those you reject. Cooperation is more productive in practical terms. Follow the lead of Newton, and find some giants on whose shoulders you will stand.

11 Jean-Pierre Protzen and David J. Harris, *The Universe of Design: Horst Rittel's Theories of Design and Planning*. New York: Routledge, 2010.

12 This, indeed, is one of the fundamental premises on which this book is built. In research design, there is no definitive formulation of a research problem. And this lack of a right answer is part of why methods are limited: you can't apply a method until you have defined the problem.

13 When I say "should," it is a pragmatic recommendation: the motivation for clear expression of ideas is based on the value of that ability for practicing research and for communicating about research.

14 Grammar is important, but it's not as important as the ideas. Be critical of the ideas.

15 If you think your prose isn't elegant enough, practice! It will get better.

16 Admittedly, some lawyers and academics seek to obfuscate, but for the moment I'll leave such deceptive purposes out of the question. It is true that the attempt to deceive or confuse does lead to bad writing, but so does lack of ability. As a basic principle, I suggest the common adage, do not attribute to malice that which can be explained by stupidity.

17 It's not a requirement, but it definitely is a valuable skill!

18 For that matter, one of the central motivations for this book was different ways of defining "literature review," which can be either a process or a written product, and which can take a number of different forms in either case.

19 You can always use a different definition on a later project.

20 Actually, I'm not sure of the sources of either of these ideas. I know of Freud's pleasure/pain principle, but that's probably not the source. The biblical "spare the rod; spoil the child," is certainly about reward/punishment. Adam Smith, I suppose, might be a reasonable source for the law of supply and demand.

21 It also gives credit to authors for their work, which is an important aspect of citation, but which is not the only reason for citation.

22 After years of seeing feedback on dissertations, I would say that the worst feedback professors give is when they spend time correcting grammar.

It's not that grammar isn't important, it's just not as important as the reasoning and the argument, and if they aren't in order, then time spent on grammar is a distraction.

That being said, if you are a graduate student, finding grammatical flaws in published work might reduce your concern about grammar and give you confidence to write, knowing that grammatical mistakes happen even to published works that have (usually) gone through multiple rounds of review and revision.

Managing the literature

Having recommended a general attitude of critical confidence in reading literature, now I'm shifting to issues in the practice of reading.

There are disparate aspects of the general practice of engaging with academic literature in the process of research design. They include issues like allocation of effort, record-keeping, and other specific ways of approaching both individual pieces, and a whole body of material that you need to command to satisfy professors and other scholars who might review your work.

Many of these ideas are, I think, so obvious that they are taken for granted, and in the press of events, with a great mass of reading to be done, they are not considered. But, reusing the student driver analogy, with practice, you will take all the little issues into account, integrating them automatically into your practice. And the clearer sense of your own research destination—the project question you want to answer and the project you want to execute—the more easily you will focus on those issues of most importance to you, and the more easily you will be able to make decisions based on your practical needs.

These practical issues are presented in two chapters: first issues related to managing a whole body of literature (i.e., thinking about the large-scale conversation among scholars and the relationships between scholars), and then issues related to deep reading of individual works (individual voices in the larger conversation).

Managing an entire discourse

Focusing on the larger discourse is different from focusing on individual works. If the literature is a conversation among scholars, and each piece only a part of that conversation, then each individual work will make most sense in comparison to other related works. In a way, reading a single work is a little like hearing only one half of a telephone conversation: you can understand a lot, but, lacking half the conversation, any interpretation is uncertain. Stepping back from a focus on a single work allows you to see the larger fabric of the discourse, providing better context for the individual works.

Trying to manage a whole body of literature entails issues not relevant to reading individual works. One difficulty in trying to read a body of literature is the question of setting limits on what you read: what is included and what is not? When reading a single work, there is no question of where it begins and ends, but where does the "relevant" literature end? Another big difficulty is keeping track of what you have read. An individual work is small enough that it's generally easy to keep the important parts of the work in your memory while you work on it. With a whole discourse, even if you can limit what you want to include, you need to keep track of which parts of the discourse you have read and which you have not, and because of the amount of material and the time involved, it's easy to forget large and important parts.[1]

Reading a whole discourse takes time and involves a wide variety of ideas, both of which mean that, in addition to the danger of forgetting important material, there is the previously mentioned "danger" that you will learn something that changes the way you see the world, which might lead to reconsideration of your own project as well as re-evaluation of material that you read previously. If the tenth article you read changes how you see the world, that shift in perspective could change how you interpret the first nine articles you read. Such shifts in understanding contribute to the difficulty of keeping a good grasp on the overall body of literature. And yet, such shifts in understanding are learning: you can only avoid such shifts by rejecting all of the ideas that you read, and what's the point in reading, then? Research is a search for new understanding, and so it often leads in uncertain directions, but you need not follow all possible paths. Part of commanding a whole body of literature is understanding which ideas you want to use and which you want to avoid, and that entails reading material that you ultimately don't use (or use only as a foil to contrast with your own positions).[2]

Given the practical limits on what you can read, you need to make choices, trust what you do know, and hope for the best. When you're deep in a subject, with mountains of reading lined up, it's easy to think in terms of what you don't know, but your doubts are no foundation for a project! Remember your foundations. You may feel you have a bare grasp on the important issues, but another person would view your training as tremendous expertise.[3] The fact that you don't have all the answers doesn't mean that you're not knowledgeable, just that you don't know everything. You'll never know everything or read everything—no-one does. As you develop a sense of the wider discourse in your community, you'll be better able to judge which readings are most worth your time.

Exercises (15 minutes)

How do you feel about the general task of managing the literature in your field?

Do you have good skills that will help in that task? What skills do you think you lack? How can you acquire those skills?

Reviewing the literature

Managing the literature is a long-term general process. As you work, and as you proceed in your research, it's important to develop a sense of how your readings fit into the larger discourse from which they're drawn, and how they relate to your own positions with respect to that discourse. This is an ongoing process—as long as you're interested in reading new literature, there's an implicit need to manage that literature.

Within that general process, there might be times when you want to engage in a more structured and specific process to become acquainted with some group of literature. In this chapter, I'll call that process "reviewing the literature," though it could as well be called a "literature review."

The phrase "literature review" can mean different things, and as part of this book's interest in literature review, I want to identify distinct meanings of the phrase. In the chapters on reading, I'm looking at "literature review" as a process.

Generally speaking, the process of reviewing the literature is one of getting acquainted with publications in some area, but this does not clearly define the scope or nature of the project. There is a spectrum of formality and rigor along which literature review processes lie, and choosing a suitable scope would depend on your purpose in some specific context.

Some reviews are informal. You might, for example, choose to do a brief literature review before attending a lecture given by a prominent scholar in your field. Such a review might involve looking at a few of the scholar's own works, as well as, perhaps, a few other recent works in that specific area. It might be the work of an afternoon, done casually, driven primarily by the desire to make the lecture more interesting.

Slightly more rigor might go into contacting a professor to request support for your work. In that case, you might be interested in reviewing their work—both to ensure that you do want to work with them, and to aid you in making an intellectual connection with them.[4]

At the formal end of the rigor and formality spectra might be a research project that carefully analyzes a body of literature in search of some insight. A formal literature review might try to aggregate results of many studies on a specific issue—for example, if there are many published clinical studies about the efficacy of some treatment, a formal, systematic review would be used to seek larger patterns of results (e.g., do most studies show positive results or not?). Or, for example, you might choose to review a set of publications for their use of method: how often do the selected articles violate accepted standards of research? Again, a study like this would depend on formal methods to generate strong conclusions. Works of this scope might be publishable projects in their own right, provided that they are of sufficient rigor and formality including clearly defined criteria for inclusion/ exclusion and a clearly defined method of analysis.

If you are designing a research project, doing a review of the literature can be helpful, but it can also be highly problematic, depending on the status of your project design. Basically, the better defined your project, the more useful a literature review process might be. This, I think, might seem counter-intuitive.

The common-sense view, I think, would be that if you are not certain of what you are doing, then a literature review is a good place to start: you review a wide range of ideas to help narrow down your interest. By contrast, if your project is already well-defined, then there seems to be little need for a literature review.

But if your project is only generally defined, then a literature review can become a massive project, which takes a lot of time and suggests many different directions to pursue. If you have not made a commitment to a project, such a review can significantly interfere with making the necessary commitment. Without some clearly defined project, you're doing exploratory reading, for which there is no real limit, and during which you can always find compelling new questions. The looser the definition of your project, the easier it is to find many different directions for exploration, which can lead into the literature review trap of needing to read "just one more article."

By contrast, if you have clearly and carefully defined a project, it is easier to limit the literature that would be involved in a review, and easier to read that literature instrumentally—looking to use it as a tool to support your project. For every aspect of the project that you define, you can do a focused review of literature on that point. Doing a sequence of literature reviews on separate issues may feel like a lot of work, but in comparison to reading generally before you start to define your own project, it's much more restrictive. And it's also responsive to what you have learned along the way.

To complete the process of research design, reviewing new literature may be less effective than working on the readings you already know. When it comes to writing a dissertation, the crucial task is designing and completing the project, so allocate your effort to the research design, not to reading more literature. Of course, this is context dependent. If you have spent the last year designing and you feel like you're committed, then it might make sense to carry out a review focused specifically on new publications just to make sure that no-one has published anything that would force you to change your project.[5]

Exercises (10 minutes)

What kinds of literature review would help you with your research project? Are they big literature reviews or small ones?

Record keeping

Good records help. Ideally, scholars keep records of everything they read throughout their academic career, so that, when it comes time for writing a dissertation or thesis, they already have a database or file of notes about a whole body of literature at hand to draw upon for their dissertation or thesis research process. If you are one such scholar, I commend you. I was not, and I've known many others who were not. But good records help.

Record keeping is hard, however, and cannot replace the crucial work of defining your own project. One dimension of the literature review trap is spending a great deal of time and effort learning to keep records at the expense of working on your own project. Record-keeping efforts, therefore, must not become a distraction.

Practical details of record keeping are outside my interest—there are good tools and good discussions of record keeping and record-keeping systems, and because record-keeping tools change so quickly, discussion of any specific tool would date this book.

Different tools work for different people—whether you use the latest cutting-edge bibliography software or some old-fashioned technique like a ring binder or notecard/index card file is a matter of choice.

Whatever tool you choose, the main burden lies in keeping the records updated and in a form that helps you use the material, and the real value lies in how you understand the issues of importance, both with respect to your own ideas and to those of others in the scholarly discourse. It's nice that software can manage the bibliographic details and formatting, but there is no software (yet) that will automatically record your new ideas in all their richness, including how a new idea might influence your relationship to some other idea you found important in the past.[6]

From the perspective of designing a research project, what is crucial about reading is how the work relates to your own project: does it support what you're doing? Does it reveal flaws in what you're doing? Or is it irrelevant to your own work? You need to make those decisions, and it would be ideal to keep records of those decisions. But, again, the ideal and the practical diverge.

Entering all those ideas into a record-keeping system would take time and effort, and some balance must be found in the practice. You want useable records, but you still want to work on designing your own project. The process of record keeping should not be so tedious that it significantly limits your ability to read the discourse. If your reading routine includes 15 minutes to update records of each new piece you read, including notes on the work's significance (in addition to the time you have to spend to actually read the piece itself), that time can really add up in comparison to a routine where only a minute is spent recording publication data, but you end up with more detailed records. Finding the right balance is personal and context-dependent. Good records can save you hassles later and help you get a grasp on large bodies of literature, but it takes time and effort that could be spent elsewhere (reading new material, or, better, working on your own project), and old records that were written from last year's perspective may be little help if your views have changed this year.

Record-keeping systems should support the development of a productive research process, not keep the researcher from developing new work. If your record-keeping plans are keeping you from focusing on your own research, change them. Read. Write. Develop your own ideas. Don't get bogged down in administrative detail describing other people's work.[7]

Exercises (15 minutes)

What are your current record-keeping practices? Do you feel they are effective? What are their strengths and weaknesses?

Do you want to change those practices in the future? What changes would you make?

How much time do you spend on record keeping?

Do you want to adopt a computerized record-keeping tool? If so, do you know which one? What are your options? What are the pros and cons?

Using what you have read

By the time you start a dissertation or independent research project, it is likely that you have read many things. If you are at the point of beginning a dissertation/thesis project, chances are good that you have already demonstrated a fairly impressive array of knowledge about the scholarship in your field; at least enough to convince your professors that you have a sufficient foundation. To what extent do you rely on the past reading that got you to this point?

It's crucial to practice using what you have already read, because if you don't, reading becomes a treadmill: if you don't use what you read to build foundations for your work, then additional readings will not move you any closer to your goal. If you're not building a foundation today, using what you have read in the past, how will that change tomorrow, or the next day? Waiting for the perfect source is a risky strategy. Maybe you will happen upon a perfect source at some point in the future. But what if you don't? If, instead, you build upon what you have already read, you may not have a perfect source, but you may be able to patch together a reasonable foundation by using pieces abstracted from a variety of sources.

Using what you have already read is not just a matter of looking back into the specific sources that have most inspired and guided you—though that would be at the heart of using what you already know. In addition to the works that influence you the most, you have at least a passing familiarity with other works. All the works that you have read and decided not to use—they may not be central to your research, but they are useful as resources that can help you set the context for your work. Some of the works that you have previously set aside because you disagree with them might be recruited into service as foils for describing your work. Other works may mostly seem irrelevant to your project, but can help you situate yourself in a field as part of a quick one-sentence "other approaches have been used" comment that allows you to show that you are familiar with a body of literature related to yours. Not everything you have ever read will be worth using, but making yourself conscious of the range of materials that you already know can help you find a foundation in what you do know, instead of searching for something new.

Getting a sense of the literature you already know ought to be one of your first steps in managing the literature. What do you know best? What have you read? Can you identify any heroes and villains? What is worth your time? It is worth your time to think about what you have already read, and whether any of it can provide a foundation for your interests. Only then can you really start to use the literature effectively.

Exercises (20 minutes)

Describe some issue important in your research in your own words and without looking for references. Focus on the dynamics/situations that interest you. What are the important aspects of that dynamic/situation? (5 minutes)

Look back at what you have written, sentence by sentence, and try to remember where those ideas came from. Did they come from personal experience, from something someone told you, from a reading, or from some other source? (15 minutes)

Finding and selecting literature

You're not going to read everything, so what are you going to read? Speaking generally, you'll find sources that you *could* read, then you'll select some that you intend to read, and then, if you're like most of us, you'll actually read an even smaller set.

Finding literature

There are many techniques for finding literature, from searching online to browsing shelves at a library to talking with friends, and chances are you can find plenty to read, so I'll just make a few comments and try not to say too much that is obvious. My general recommendation is to choose fewer sources; you can always search for more.

Here are a few suggestions with respect to different sources.

Searches on scholarly databases potentially turn up hundreds of results—especially if your searching tactics include looking at related ideas. The great danger is the surfeit of potential sources. Don't overwhelm yourself drawing from such sources. You can always go back to the database. One way to keep from overwhelming yourself is to limit yourself to the past year or so. A review of most recent works can give a useful indication of issues currently of interest to scholars in your field.

Suggestions from professors can be an odd thing: many people have some emotional resistance when a professor recommends a work. I know that when I was a student, I often felt a certain resentment about readings recommended by professors because I already felt so far behind in the list of what I hoped to read. I have spoken with many other students who have felt something similar. They have told me they felt overloaded with reading already, and when professors suggested readings, it was overwhelming. Nonetheless, suggestions from professors are very useful as the professors know your work, and think their recommendation relates in some way (they may not always be right, but the recommendation gives some insight into their thinking about your work).

Suggestions from other readings are often useful. Many good sources can be found in the reference lists in the work you read. This may seem obvious to you, but in my experience, many think about the literature search almost exclusively in terms of searching large, comprehensive databases, whether at libraries or online. The advantage of sources taken from the reference list of something you read is that they have been selected and vetted by an author whose work you respect. This does not guarantee the quality of the cited work, but it guarantees that at least one scholar found it valuable when they were trying to communicate their own ideas.

Setting limits and finishing projects

You're not going to read everything, so the questions become: how much are you going to read, and what *must* you read? These questions can best be answered relative to specific projects and practical ends. Set goals that you can accomplish and that allow you to finish projects in a reasonable time.

Searching is a time-consuming activity

Don't spend too much time searching, and especially not early in the process. How many possible readings do you need to find before you actually read them? Start reading and writing. As you develop your own voice and define your own project, let your searches be guided by what you learn in the process.

Make a list; keep focused on the most important items on it

In the process of finding literature you will implicitly or explicitly develop a list of what to read next. Given that you want to manage the literature, I think it's worth the time to keep and update an explicit master list of possible readings. If you find possible articles online, add them to the list. Don't be intimidated by the list growing long, just keep focused on the next reading you want to do. This leads to the question of selecting what to read from the list of possible readings.

Selecting literature

Granting that you already have your foundation of things you've already read, and that you are going to be able to find more things you *could* read than you will actually read, how do you choose among the possible readings? How will you decide what to read next?

I suggest using a prioritization and scheduling perspective. If you look at what you *could* read, or what you *should* read—if your selection principle is guided by theoretical issues (i.e., you say "I need to read material related to subject X")—then you are likely to designate a fairly large body of material to read. That large stack of reading can be overwhelming. But you'll only read one thing at a time.[8] Instead, focus on the most important thing to read: what are you going to read next?

You can maintain a list of possible readings (or a pile of books to read, or a folder filled with digital articles, etc.), but however big those lists get, you can always focus on the question of what to read next. Focusing on choosing what to read next allows you to avoid feeling overwhelmed by the size of any list of reading. You don't need to read the whole list, you only have to choose one thing to read! And don't get hung up on making the perfect choice. Make a choice and focus on that reading; don't spend time vacillating.

Prune your lists

It's really easy to make a long list of things to read, to print a huge stack of articles, or to borrow a mountain of books from the library. Easy on a certain emotional level, anyway. Making long lists and collecting a vast array of material to read later can help manage anxiety about dealing with a whole body of literature. But that pile can become an emotional burden. For a lot of people, the unread backlog weighs on them as an unfinished task.

To avoid being overwhelmed by massive lists of possible readings, don't be afraid to prune your lists to keep them short. You want the lists to be an aid, not a burden. If your lists of what to read next (or piles of books or articles to read) are so big that it takes hours to make a decision, and you're burdened with guilt for all the things that you're not reading, then your lists are too long.

Don't worry about letting things fall off the list. If something has been on the list for a long time and it's not a top priority, let it go! If you feel that something is a top priority and it remains on your list unread, you need to reconsider. If you're resisting reading the work, make a choice: read it or drop it from the list. Think about why you don't want to read it. Is it really necessary? If your professor has told you that you must cite the work in your own work, then you have to read it—so commit to it. Focus your attention on the things you are going to read.

Reprioritize, but keep an eye on completing projects

You learn as you go, so it makes sense to reprioritize your lists every time you're looking for something to read. But remember to keep your reading separate from any specific research project. You may have a personal intellectual revolution (that's what learning is!), but don't let new ideas block the completion of old projects. Don't give up a project that is a long way toward completion just because you found some great new idea. Save the new idea for the next project.

Exercises (10–20 minutes)

Are you able to find works to read? Too few, too many, or just enough? If too many, how will you prune your lists? What tools will you use to select those that you spend your time reading? If too few, how can you add to your lists?

Does your list of possible readings grow faster than your list of completed readings? What does that say about your allocation of time between reading and searching? What does that say about the amount of time spent reading each work?

Accept practical limits

As previously mentioned, many people get stuck in a cycle of saying, "I don't know enough; I need to read more." If you have a habit of skeptical doubt—which is appropriate for a scholar—then it's very easy to see the need to learn more and read more. And it's really, really easy to find some other work that might be relevant and important. This task has no logical limit: each new reading leads to more reading, but, practically, there is only so much you can read. You need to have confidence to say, "Despite the limits of my knowledge, I can develop my own research ideas." Whatever your situation, you want to keep an eye on the practical dimensions of your work in order to finish your project—and that means doing stuff other than reading.

I've known people in professional programs to say, "This is my one chance to do academic work, so I want to make it really good," thus justifying more and more work. And I've known people in academic programs who said, "This is the beginning of my career, so I have to do a really good job to impress people," and they go searching for what others have said and defer their own research. If you are reading without writing about your own ideas and projects, then you're spending too much time reading. For that matter, if you are reading more than you are writing, then you're spending too much time reading.

How much reading is necessary? That's a question whose answer depends on context. What you "need" to read as a scholar depends on what interests you and what you choose to do, and it also depends on the people with whom you work. What will satisfy your professors? What will satisfy other members of your community, like the peer reviewers at a journal? Developing your own work and ideas should be central, but it's worth keeping in mind what others will expect and accept, too.[9]

Pragmatically, what you "need" to know is whatever you're capable of learning with a reasonable expenditure of resources. If you've been working hard and having success as a student then, on a certain level, most of what you "need" to know is what you already know. If you can convince your department that you're ready to begin your independent research project (your dissertation), doesn't that mean that they think you're ready to begin without doing a whole lot of extra reading? Trust yourself and what you have already accomplished. And take a chance.

How much do you need?
This is a thought experiment—an exercise in imagination.

Can you imagine justifying a study using only one piece of literature? Would your professors accept that? What would it take for that one study to suffice?

What if you read an article that was very close to what you want to study, and it suggested a good follow-up study that you could execute? If that article covered all the necessary bases—good explanation of theory, method, etc.—could you do a research study that used the same theoretical and methodological framework and didn't rely on other work?

Practically speaking, a dissertation depending on a single source would probably not satisfy professors or reviewers, but you wouldn't interact with that single article without other literature being drawn in, anyway. Firstly, the article you were looking at would almost certainly use multiple sources, and you would thus use those sources indirectly even if you didn't go read them yourself. Secondly, you understand what you read in terms of what you've already learned, and so you're drawing on that larger set of ideas from your previous education to guide your interpretation of that single work.

You won't be able to get away with reading only one thing, but then you wouldn't be in graduate school if you had only read one thing. When it's time to do your dissertation, try to focus your efforts on defining a project you can complete, and read only what helps with that goal. What is the absolute minimum you need to read to complete your own work? Try to develop your study with as few new sources as possible, rely on your past readings where possible, and see what results.

Research is an ongoing process, so you can always read more. If you develop your own research using as few sources as possible, you may finish sooner. There is nothing stopping you from doing more reading after you finish a project (or while you're still working on it). And if someone tells you that you absolutely must include a specific source, then you can always read it.

Exercises (15 minutes)

What are your practical limits? What are your practical limits on a daily basis? What about on a weekly basis? How much time do you have? How much time does it take to effectively process a single source from the literature in your field? How many such works can you read while also spending time to develop your own project?

Seek efficiency: issues in selecting literature

Scholars are expected to have a functional familiarity with a massive reading list. A scholar is expected to understand the main ideas used in their field. But very few specific works are utterly necessary, provided a scholar has a solid foundation and familiarity with the wider literature. No scholar is expected to have read *everything*,[10] but scholars are certainly expected to be able to discuss the ideas that shape the field, points of major debate, and the major scholars who have defined or used the most important concepts. The better you can see patterns in the literature—similarities between different authors—the easier it becomes to discuss your work with respect to the literature as a whole.

The field of literature

The field of literature is the published manifestation of the conversations among scholars on issues of relevance. As such, the relationships between the different voices—the different people—are important. These relationships are often discussed in spatial terms. "How do you position yourself with respect to other scholars in the field?" is a question that I was asked as a student, and that I have seen many others asked when trying to write scholarly works (especially literature reviews). Just speaking of the "*field* of literature" or "*field* of study" lexically draws on a spatial metaphor. It is a useful metaphor that uses spatial thinking to describe relationships in the literature in terms of a physical location.

This metaphor works very well with the idea that the research literature represents a conversation among scholars, in which they try to add to or correct the ideas that have already been accepted by the research community. Conversations in groups of people (communities) often play out in a spatial form: groups of people gathered together arrange themselves spatially according to the people with whom they speak, with each subgroup representing a different part of the larger set of ideas being discussed in the group as a whole. Social groups do this, as, for example, when small groups form at people's parties. Political bodies— congresses, parliaments—often arrange themselves spatially according to ideology.

Imagine the scholars in a field literally standing in a field. How would they arrange themselves? Different groups and clusters would form on some shared subject of discussion, even if there was not uniform agreement within the cluster. One can imagine different clusters facing off against each other at certain times—for example, if psychotherapists were on the field, the people using psychodynamic theories might face off against the cognitive behavioral people and have a shared debate about whether to use psychodynamic therapies or cognitive behavioral therapies. We can also imagine many deciding that they don't want to participate in that debate, and they walk off to have some other conversation. Some might be psychodynamicists who want to talk with other psychodynamicists—perhaps forming two or more groups that agree on psychodynamics, but have some theoretical debate within that agreement. Others might be cognitive behaviorists who want to talk with other cognitive behaviorists, to debate some point of cognitive behavioral theory. We can imagine a variety of individual responses, each playing out as an actual conversation that entails spatial relationships as people come together to talk, or turn away from each other to end conversations. In this "scholars on a field" thought experiment, we might say that positioning yourself with respect to the scholars in the field is done by thinking about the conversations you might have with the different scholars you have read: with whom would you speak, whether to agree or to debate, and whom would you ignore?

Recognizing these different conversations allows greater efficiency in reading and managing the literature because it allows you to skip reading a lot of material (and later to skip writing about it). In a way, you can imagine talking to any of the scholars in a large field, if for no other reason than that you're both in the same field: "We both do education"; "We both study history"; etc. With any single scholar, you may find more or less agreement: "I do mathematics education and you do literature education" may signal the end of a conversation, or it may be bridged by some other idea: "we both believe in the same educational paradigm, even though in different subjects." It can be valuable to identify the ground that you do share with people with whom you otherwise disagree. A Freudian and cognitive behaviorist might not be able to agree on much, but they both agree on the value of talk therapy.

To manage a large field of literature, look for the web of debate and the different positions taken by scholars with respect to each other. Seeing the large relationships that exist outside any single work can facilitate selecting, prioritizing, and allocating effort to specific works.

One needs to read some works more closely than others. To manage the literature, it makes sense to spend more time working closely with those works that are most valuable, and less time with works of lesser import. Admittedly, it isn't always possible to know whether a work is valuable until you've read it closely—there are certainly works of great intellectual value that are so hard to read and understand that their significance may not be obvious when skimming during the process of quickly reviewing many works. Some works justify the time, even if they initially seem impenetrable, or even incoherent.[11] But all the same, your work process can be more efficient by making good judgments about how much time to dedicate to any work.

Exercises (10 minutes)

How can you maintain a balance between reading works closely and reviewing the wider mass of literature in your field? What are your concerns? On which side of the balance are you: too much deep reading and not enough general review, or too much general review and not enough deep reading?

Iterative reading: from quick reviews toward deep reading

As I said, not all works deserve the same attention. Efficiency can be found by making good decisions about where to dedicate effort. Roughly speaking, you can skim works to get a general idea of what is in them, or you can read deeply to know them well. From a more fine-grained perspective, there is a continuum between reading closely and skimming. To judge which works deserve significant attention, you can engage with a single work repeatedly with increasing effort. You start with only a little information, and a little effort, and for works that seem worth continued engagement, you go back for more information on a few successive readings.

In the first cycle, you spend only a minute or two looking at a work. In the next cycle, several minutes are spent. In the third, perhaps a quarter of an hour. After that, you move on to a deeper reading, which is the subject of the following chapter.

Managing the literature well is not just having an understanding of the people and their theories, it is a task demanding resources. The point of iterated engagement at progressively deeper levels is to create greater efficiency in your overall use of the literature by minimizing time spent on less valuable works while also helping you get a better sense of the wide scope of ideas in the field.

These points are not exactly novel, but I have known plenty of people who would do a search, and immediately collect a whole stack of articles, and then sit down intending to read them all. For most of us, that's not efficient: it doesn't use easily available information to limit your effort. Just because a title showed up in your search, it doesn't mean you want to read the work (as I said, my points are not exactly novel).

Successive rounds of increasing engagement

I talked previously of keeping a list of what to read next and of pruning that list to save time. You want to cull out different works based on the differential value of their content. Some works are more relevant to your work than others, and you want to spend time with the most relevant material. Instead of one simple skim to see if you want to do a deeper read, take a series of increasingly close looks to both familiarize yourself with the work as part of the larger "landscape," as well as to decide where to spend more time.

Generally, works deserve a deeper look if they are *directly* relevant to what you're doing, by which I mean that you think, "I will use this in my work."[12] Thinking that you *could* use a work may be too generous. You're looking for works that serve an important purpose with respect to your research design choices. Even if you are not currently committed to a specific research project, you can ask yourself whether you would like to use something you read as a guide in setting up research. Is there a theoretical point you would like to explore? A suggestion for future research you would like to follow? A methodological approach you would like to emulate?

Practically speaking, there is a second important criterion for a student to consider: will a professor demand that you know a work? You may not think a work is directly relevant, but if you know that one of your professors is going to expect you to know it, then that work should get deeper review, but still go through the successive passes of review. In such a situation, you might focus on looking for reasons that your professor wants you to use it and reasons you don't want to use it: that way you can manage its inclusion in your work, or develop a good argument for why you're not going to use it, if you decide that's appropriate.

In any event, with almost all works, start with quick passes, and if the work meets sufficient criteria, move on to deeper levels of engagement. In a way, each of these reviews deserves focused attention, not just a quick, "uh, yeah, looks interesting" or "no thanks." Try to explicate the reason the work is or is not worth greater attention. The first pass does not require actually accessing the work: it focuses on the publication data found in search results. For works with abstracts, you can make a second pass on the abstract, which often can be accessed without actually acquiring the work itself. Later passes can focus on a table of contents (for a book), or on a bibliography or on some other specific portion of the work—these may require getting a copy of the work (an increased investment of your time and perhaps money), but they don't require reading the whole thing.

> **Exercises** (variable time)
>
> Try some of the practices described above. Look at a stack of articles (or a screenful of search responses) and sort through them. Or look at a specific article's abstract or contents for evidence of whether it is worth a deeper read.

First iteration: title and publication information

First engagement is with the title, author and publication information, including year. This is what you'll find in most searches (whether online, in lists of works cited, or, formerly, in the now-antiquated card catalogs of libraries).

This first set of information is often treated very casually. I think a lot of people just list all the titles found for later retrieval and reading—I know I've done this. But in order to get a grasp of the body of literature as a whole, you can benefit by taking *more* time with this initial review. Don't just copy the title from the search results on to your "to read" list because the title sounds good. Spend a minute or two. Consider titles and other publication information with some care and try to rank the quality of the works.

1. Title:

Having identified a potential source's title, you can ask several questions: What aspects of the title relate to your interest? How closely does it align with your interests? What are the points of difference? What are the points of similarity? Titles are not always clearly indicative of all the relevant contents (which is a motivation for newer publications having "keywords"), but titles often contain crucial information that would enable a good decision on whether or not to spend more time with the work.[13]

2. Author(s)

While it is inappropriate to judge the value of any claim based on the speaker (the rhetorical *ad hominem* fallacy), it is useful to consider the author as a criterion to judge whether to read a work. Works by a given author will generally be of similar quality, and will generally follow similar schools of thought, so an additional source in the same vein as something you have valued might be worth the effort, or might be redundant. And an additional source from an author whose work has not been valuable is a quick sign to direct your attention elsewhere. So take time to consider the author. Have you seen other works by the author(s)? Have these works been useful? Have you seen this author cited? If so, by whom? The more a given scholar's work appears, the greater the value it will provide in terms of engaging the larger scholarly discourse. Using well-known ideas and sources in your own work—whether as hero or villain—helps readers in your field understand how your work relates to their own ideas and to ideas in the field in general. And if you are not already familiar with a name, it's still useful to give it enough attention to help you remember it if you see it later. Names that frequently show up in your searches are usually worth attention, if only to understand why they keep on turning up in your searches.

3. Year

Many people will put a lot of emphasis on the year of publication. I have known many students who were criticized for using sources that were "too old." Some universities have explicit policies governing recency of citations. While I don't believe that good ideas go out of date, there is a very real value in seeing the chronological development of the literature: the temporal element is relevant in understanding how different ideas and authors relate to each other. If you are under time pressure (and who isn't?), it may be useful to allow the date to be a factor in deciding whether to examine an article more deeply or not.

As a rule of thumb, you might limit yourself by looking at older works[14] only if they are cited in a more current source that you respect.

4.   Other publication information

Some other publication information can be valuable. Different publishers and different journals have characters and qualities that, with reading, may become familiar to you. If a work is published by a journal or publisher that you either respect or disrespect, that can help you make a decision. By thinking about the publication information when you're reviewing titles, you will start to get a sense of which journals and publishers have work that you value.

Be critical when reviewing lists of search results. Instead of making long lists of titles for later reading, make shorter lists of works for a second round of review. You want to cull your lists, but, by spending a little more time, even the titles that you cull from your list help you get a sense of the community of researchers in which you participate.

Exercises (15 minutes)

Do a search for something related to your research. (Use an academic search engine, not just a general web search.)

How many titles did you turn up?

How many of those titles can you review for the criteria listed in this section in 10 minutes?

Were any of the authors familiar to you?

Were any of the works worth a second pass to review the abstract?

Second iteration: abstract

After the preliminary review of title, author, and publication data, the next step is the abstract, when available. Not all books will have an abstract, but some other brief description of the work may be available—most books will have some promotional text, which may not be quite as academic or focused as an abstract, but might be useful. Whenever possible, give the abstract a read before committing to reading an entire work. As with consideration of title, author, and publication data, a little extra attention to the abstract can save effort in the long run. It's much easier to download an article from a journal site than it is to read the abstract closely and carefully, so this is another stage at which there can be a temptation to just make a stack of articles to read closely later. Reading an entire article can often take multiple hours, whereas reading most abstracts closely and carefully can be done in about 10 minutes, with some few complicated yet valuable ones warranting more time. Again, this immediate investment of time can spare you the effort of acquiring and reading the whole article, while still giving you valuable information about the general discourse in your field.

Abstracts can reveal several significant concerns that can inform the decision of whether to read a work more deeply:

1. Motivation (or significance)
2. Theoretical commitments/theoretical framework

    a. Ideas
    b. Sources

3. Methods
4. Concepts, definition of terms, and operationalization of constructs
5. Conclusions

Taking each of these in turn:

1. Motivation

Most abstracts will include a sentence that explains why the work is of value. This may be couched in terms of the significance of the work, or it may be a more direct statement of motivation (e.g., "This work arose out of a concern with ...").

2. Theoretical commitments and theoretical framework

Authors will implicitly or explicitly express the theoretical framework that shapes their work. One cannot express an academic interest without relying on a structure of ideas (premises), starting with the basic definition of the subject (which I discuss separately, below). In looking at an abstract, you want to look for the ideas that structure the work, and structure the reasoning. Additionally, an abstract may explicitly state a commitment to the works of specific authors.

3. Methods

Abstracts will include some basic description of the method used—using the term "method" loosely here to include any approach, whatever its character: close reading of texts, as done in humanities, or logical argumentation, as found in philosophy, are parallel to the research method used in an empirical study. Whether a work uses strict empirical methods or not, there is some general principle that guides the discussion (it is to be hoped) that can be identified as a "method." What are these methods? Are they any good?[15] How do they relate to the questions asked by the author? How do they relate to your project (or at least to the interests that led you to the work)? Can you use their methods in any way?

4. Concepts, definition of terms, and operationalization of constructs

Crucial in any theoretical framework is the definition of terms. What are the concepts and constructs used? How is the subject defined and delimited? While abstracts do not typically include detailed explicit definitions of terms, the way a word is used will implicitly define it.

5. Conclusions

In addition to the foundational aspects that define the work, what conclusions do the authors draw from the study? Abstracts do usually state basic conclusions. Are those conclusions interesting and provocative?

Given that abstracts contain a lot of useful information, it makes sense to spend 10 minutes or more analyzing a promising abstract. By giving extra time to the abstract, you can glean a good deal of crucial information about a work and its place in the wider conversation in your field, without committing the time necessary for a complete examination of the entire work.

If you've gotten through the abstract and decided the work is worth more time, you might consider a couple of next steps that still avoid a complete reading: reviewing the table of contents and introduction along with a rapid skim of the whole body; and looking over the bibliography.

Exercises (10 minutes)

Pick an abstract. Work through it as suggested above. Judging from the abstract, would you use that work? Why or why not? Is it worth a deeper read? Why or why not?

Third iteration: single sections

By the time you get to a third iteration, you're moving toward reading the work deeply. However, in this section I suggest a few possible engagements with a piece of writing that aren't yet getting into the full details, and that can be done relatively quickly while also returning some useful information.

Third pass (A): table of contents, introduction, conclusion, skimming

For books, which may not have abstracts, you may often be able to see the table of contents and the introduction without acquiring the entire book. Introductions to academic work generally are intended to give the reader a picture of the work as a whole, so reading the introduction closely will usually give a good idea of the whole work—its sources, its theoretical commitments, its conclusions. A review of the table of contents will also help you get a sense of the shape of their story.

Before deep reading, you will want to skim the main body and perhaps look more closely at the conclusion to help you get a sense of the main ideas and themes of the work. All of these should be done with an eye toward getting an overview of the whole. These are some final steps to take before making the commitment to read a work closely: even if the work has passed your earlier checks, you may still want to avoid close reading. If you do each of these three passes for a work, you will have gathered a pretty good idea of the work's concerns in any event.

Third pass (B): bibliography

Alternatively, the next place to turn your attention can be the reference list: what sources are being used? And, more importantly, which sources are good for you? I discuss reading bibliographies in greater detail later, but the greater your general familiarity with the larger discourse in your field, the easier it is to use the bibliography to understand the ideas being used; and the more time you spend scanning bibliographies, the better your sense of the larger literature will be.[16] Knowing who an author has chosen to reference, gives some sense of where that author is positioned with respect to others in the literature.

Doing everything described in the third pass (both A and B), could take only 15 minutes—a good target, because it allows you to go through a large number of pieces in a relatively short time. You might want to take an hour for a work of particular interest, but that's essentially the decision to do a deeper reading.

On a certain level, what I'm suggesting here is finding a spot where you're not just adding to a list of works that you'll look at later, you're giving enough attention to each piece that you can remember looking at it—enough that you could honestly tell a peer or professor: "Yes, I saw that," and perhaps make a cogent comment regarding what you saw, without having to claim detailed knowledge.

This level of reading is intended to give you a sense of the wide range of work and ideas in your field: it's a focus on the whole fabric of research and theory in the community. It's not attention on any but the most general theoretical points.

Exercises (15 minutes)

Pick a work. Spend about 10 minutes checking the introduction, conclusion, and table of contents (if there is one). Did you gain any new insights?

Spend about 5 minutes checking the bibliography. Did you see any familiar names? Did you see any names or references that would be worth your time?

Project 4: managing the literature

To manage the literature effectively, you want to use what you have already read, and you want to plan future readings judiciously. This project has two tasks to help with that: an inventory of what you have read previously, and an assessment of what you need to read in the future.

Part 1: what have you read?

Look back at old course syllabuses and records you have kept. Check your bookshelves and files (both real and computerized). Make a list of works you have read in the past. For each, consider: does it have any ideas you use? Could it help you with your project?

Categorize the entries in the list in some rough way—perhaps, the stuff you already use, the stuff that you might use, and the stuff that you won't use.

Get a sense of the foundations from which you are building. All the material you have read in the past is part of that foundation, even if you don't remember it well (of course, it might not be a big part of the foundation, but still, it's worth recognizing as part of what has gotten you to where you are now).

Part 2: what do you need to read?

What is your current list of planned future readings?

How much time would it take to read all of those works?

Which are the most important for your own research?

Are there any entries on that list that can be removed for intellectual reasons (e.g., not relevant or tangential)?

Are there any entries on that list that can be removed for practical purposes (e.g., time management considerations, redundancy)?

Notes

1 In a way, the most important parts of the discourse are those that you remember. As discussed earlier, I recommend trying to build on the material you know, which is likely the material you know best. But still, people forget important stuff. That's why they keep records. In any event, if you read dozens or hundreds of sources over the course of a year or more, you probably won't remember all of the details you've read.

2 When I say "don't use," I mean in the general sense of rejecting important theoretical considerations. As, for example, with a post-colonial critic who does not use the theoretical concerns of other schools of criticism. Or, for example, an economist who accepts market theory and rejects Marxist theory. At a different level—in terms of use of specific citations in writing—there will often be material that you cite for the specific purpose of rejecting the theoretical claim, or that you don't use explicitly (i.e., cite) but do accept theoretically.

3 Consider, by analogy, the medical profession: MDs are far more knowledgeable about medical issues than the average person, and still MDs often have trouble diagnosing problems or finding treatments to known problems. Medical doctors, of course, have "practices." Indeed, any career that involves difficult decisions in practical situations is a practice that shares characteristics with research in the need to gather and analyze information. The researcher's tools—especially the ability to read, to process/analyze information, and to put that information to use—are tools that can serve the MD, the clinical therapist, the teacher, the architect, the engineer, and so on. Even the cook, to stay with my earlier analogy, benefits from the ability to read and process culinary literature.

4 It's somewhat outside the ideal of disinterested academia to note that on a personal level, people are often flattered when others know their work. And flattery can influence people to be more helpful.

5 Of course, there's a huge difference between reading to make sure that no-one has published anything that would force you to change your work and reading to explore all the important new ideas on a subject. The first only requires checking for things that specifically relate to your work, while the second calls for a deeper reading.

6 In the end, the records of your own ideas—what you have learned, how you learned it, why you believe it—are what really matter. Your ideas are what make your work original.

   It should also be noted that the amount of time you would spend on bibliographic stuff is generally limited: fixing citations by hand may be a big annoyance, but it's a matter of hours or days of work. In the context of a project that can take months or years, that's nothing. By contrast, if you have problems defining and proposing a project, you can lose months or more.

7 With an emphasis on "don't get bogged down." Some attention to administrative detail will make your life easier in the long run. Keep it in balance.

8 At least in the most granular level: at any given second in which you're actually reading, you're only reading one thing. You may be in the middle of eighteen different books or articles, but still, you only work on one thing at a time.

9 And remember: what a professor suggests is different from what they will accept.

10 Despite horror stories of professors infuriated that a student couldn't speak in detail on some obscure source, I think it rather more common that professors will want to talk about what you have read than what you haven't.

11 There are other clues to the importance of a work: you may not be able to read or understand a certain work easily, but if you see that work being cited by many others, then you have a reason to pursue that work in greater depth.

12 Or even "I must use this." Or, if you're making explicit the ideas that you use, "I already use this in my work."

13 Remember: deciding not to read something is not a decision set in stone. If you decide to ignore a work for the present, you can always go back and read it later. This is another reason to err on the side of stricter limits on what you plan to read: time spent reading unnecessary works can't be recovered, but you can always read something if need arises. And if a work is really valuable, there's a good chance it will show up in more than one place, so dropping a title off your "to read" list incurs little risk because you'll likely get another opportunity to consider that title.

14 What counts as older depends on context. For empirical studies where there is a good deal of work in the last two or three years, then five

years might be old. Ten years might be a good time frame for studies in areas that get less attention. For important theoretical works, twenty years might be considered reasonably recent.

15 An abstract may only give minimal information about methods, so it may be hard to assess their methods without moving on to reading the methods section. But if there is information to critique the method, use it. This step of reviewing the abstract is meant to help you cull articles from the list of things you need to read deeply, while also giving you a sense of the wider literature.

16 Every bibliography/reference list can be viewed as the results of a search for useable sources.

Deep reading

As discussed earlier, there are different purposes for reading. These different purposes create new opportunities to return to a familiar text. In the previous chapter, I was discussing successive iterations of a work to decide whether it is worth a deeper engagement. But that process of returning to a work does not necessarily end when you decide to read a work deeply. Deep reading can also be seen as an ongoing practice more than a single endeavor. You don't just read an article once, and then you're done with it. The more a work influences you, the more likely it is that you will return to it. And each time you return to the work, you may be motivated by a new purpose.

The history of a person's interactions with a work can be extensive. It might start with assigned reading for coursework. That reading might be a struggle to understand a difficult work and to satisfy a professor. That first engagement might not even lead to a positive impression. But then, at some point in the future, the work comes back to mind and earns another reading. This time it might make more sense, and might seem important. That experience in itself might inspire a future attempt to read the work again. After that, other events might cause a return to the work: a conversation, a lecture, another reading. Until, perhaps, there is a decision to use that work as part of a research project, which leads to yet another return to the same work as it is used for a citation and source of quotations for a project proposal.

Each new return to the work is motivated by new contexts and purposes that create different foci. The first reading is an attempt to grasp main points. A reading motivated by a conversation with a professor might focus on one specific aspect. A reading motivated by something else that you read might focus on a different aspect. A reading motivated by a writer's desire to cite or even quote the work will focus very precisely on the specific issue the writer is writing about. Each of these readings could be active, concentrated efforts that take hours.[1] So "deep reading" isn't really a single event, it's more a process of integrating a work into your own research. At first you're introduced, and over time, as your own research develops and you struggle with the difficulties of theory and research design, you return to the research that makes the most sense to you as a source of help.

Earlier, I suggested a student-driver analogy for reading—details that seem overwhelming to a novice are easily handled with experience—and that analogy still holds: with practice, you do see more and more in a single reading. Nonetheless, there are many different ways that you could return to a reading to get value from it. This chapter discusses a few different perspectives that you might take while reading, such as looking for models for your own research, or looking at authors' use of style and rhetoric.

Direct models

A very good way to design a research project is to copy someone else's. If you copy what someone else did, you have a model for what you need to do, so you don't need to figure out all the difficult details yourself. But copying does entail attention to detail, so if you want to use someone else's research as a model, you need read their work closely, to see where your work and theirs might have to diverge. (To be clear, the concern here is specifically with design of a research project, and with copying research design or elements of research design. This is no problem ethically, so long as you give credit to your source. Carrying out a near-identical copy of someone else's research design is a "replication study" and sometimes valuable. This is not a suggestion that you rip off someone else's work, but that you learn to use previous research as a model for your own independent work. It's common for students in a laboratory science to copy elements of the experiments done by others in the same laboratory.)

Copying and using models can be emotionally difficult. If you want to do original work, copying others may feel like cheating. But, practically speaking, copying others makes it easier to develop research that is both academically sound and original. The research that you copy is the giant upon whose shoulders you stand in order to see a little farther. Once you have built a foundation, you add something of your own to create original work.

Practically speaking, one of the easiest ways to develop solid research is to closely copy someone else's work in all but one (or a few) crucial aspect(s). A single crucial difference is enough to make your work original, and then all the similarities with your model(s) will help your project fit into the larger research discourse.

This can be easiest and most obvious with detailed empirical studies. A study, for example, that examines some educational intervention can be imitated almost exactly and made original by focusing on a slightly different population than the previous study. A study carried out with 15-year olds, could be transformed by looking at 16-year olds, or a specific sub-group of 15-year olds (e.g., by gender, race, ethnicity, or socio-economic status). Or that study could be carried out using an altered intervention. You would, of course, want to be able to explain why these alterations of a single factor are theoretically interesting but in the right situations, such modeling could be a very effective way to develop your own research project.

For those concerned with copying, it is worth noting that, in practice, copying someone else's work precisely is very difficult, even when a replication study would be desirable.[2] For graduate students, published works are often difficult to copy because they are often the product of funded research, while graduate students typically have a more limited budget. Because of the changes that might be forced by practical limits, a scholar attempting to copy is often pushed toward originality.

A question worth asking about published work is how closely you could imitate it to good effect. There are many different specific aspects of any study that you could copy, as will be discussed in the next several pages. But here I'm asking: can you copy several different aspects at one time? Can you copy all but one? Can you do the same research in a new context and get interesting results? Can you do the same research but on a different set of data? Can you use a slightly different method to pursue the same question? How closely could you copy the works you read?

Rhetorical and stylistic models

The scholarly and scientific dimensions of a work are obviously good points for examination, both theory and method. But, as a scholar, you will be called upon to explain your work, too, which is a task that can be facilitated by looking at how others have explained their own work. Therefore, as you read, in addition to looking for theoretical and methodical models, you can also consider the rhetorical model: how do authors present ideas and try to persuade their audience?

Exercises (5 minutes, repeat for a few different works)

What is a work that you would like to copy? Why? What keeps you from copying it? What changes would you need to make to be able to copy it?

Motivation

Academia—the ivory tower—is accused of being disconnected from the real world, and many a graduate student has, I think, fallen prey to the sense that their research is meaningless. But academics actually care about the real world intensely. They care about telling stories about the world that are not fiction, and they put tremendous effort into gathering information from the real world and analyzing that information carefully. The things that motivate some scholars may not be the same things that motivate you—you may not, for example, find Hume's work so compelling that it motivates you to write a book, like it did Kant—but understanding what motivates other scholars can help you get a clearer sense of what motivates you and thus a clearer sense of your own purposes. And seeing how other authors motivate their works can also provide a model for how you can explain your own motivations to your readers.

How do scholars motivate their work? How do they justify the value of the project? Why do they think it is worthy of research? Why do they care at all? It's common to discuss "significance" of studies, or "gaps in literature"; the idea of "motivation" captures both such concerns. What has set the research and researcher in motion? What did the researcher care about? What are both the logical and emotional motivations for others? Recognizing this dimension in other works will call your own logical and emotional motivations into the forefront of your considerations, which will be useful when it's time to write about your own work.

Understanding what motivates other research provides material you can use to ground your work in the community and, when it's time to write, material you can use to convince others of the value of your own work.

Generally, motivation can be found in some sort of problem that an author wants to address. That problem may be practical—a clinical problem or a public policy problem, for example—or it may be more abstract, some sort of logical or intellectual problem observed in current theory.

Authors commonly (but not always) state their motivations near the beginning of their respective sources, because the beginning of any work is where context is being set (and, if you're thinking as a writer, it's where the audience either engages or moves on to something else). Kant's appeal to Hume (and the problems he caused), for example, makes an appeal to those readers who care about the issues raised by Hume. Discussion of motivations is not limited to the opening of works or for main themes only; it is possible to find motivations throughout the texts as scholars try to explain why they did what they did—not only why they chose the general topic, but why they chose to focus on specific aspects, why they chose specific methods, etc.

Each choice made by the author is an issue of motivation in itself. The broad choice of a topic requires motivation. The choice of method requires motivation. Each choice of variable, construct or data source requires motivation. And so on. Sorting out these threads can help guide you in making choices on similar issues: would you make the same choice as the author? Why or why not?

Additionally, we can recognize another dimension of these threads: their sources. Some motivations are related to a concrete problem in the real world; for example, the concern for public health that motivates the public health researcher. Other motivations are perhaps more purely personal or intellectual. Kant's response to Hume, for example, was motivated by his sense that Hume was wrong, not by any social concern. These motivations can be combined: a researcher can be simultaneously motivated by a social concern and an intellectual/theoretical concern. A psychologist, for example, might wish to understand the causes of a specific pathology both to help people (social motivation) and to answer unanswered questions (intellectual motivation).

Exercises (30 seconds; repeat)

What do you care about? What motivates you? What are some big motivations that guided big decisions (like your choice of topic)? What are some smaller motivations that guided smaller decisions (like your choice of some specific method or dimension of your focus)?

Audience

In discussing motivation, I said that one concern was motivating the audience to be interested in the work. Looking at the motivations expressed is one way of understanding the audience an author hopes to reach. In deep reading, looking to understand an author's audience also includes examining the way the author tries to build a form of solidarity with the desired audience. I have already suggested that as a matter of managing the literature you read critically with an eye for finding specific reasons to choose specific works while culling others from your reading list, which is the question of whether the work suits a specific audience: you. But now I am suggesting that you take the more general perspective of examining how a written work defines its audience, both as a model for your own writing and as a way of seeing the larger theoretical/discursive "landscape."

When work starts by saying, "there is a problem, and we want to address that problem," it is providing a motivation with which readers can associate.

For example, a general starting place for a scholar in public health might be, "There are high rates of pathology X (e.g., cancer), and we want to address that problem." That's a simple motivation, and it's a good place to start. But, of course, it's not necessarily a motivation that would strike all equally. Students outside public health—in education, for example—have already implicitly made the choice to work on different problems. Students in education may care about pathology X in a general sense, but it's not a concern for their chosen field of study.[3] For a student of education, "school outcomes are not good," is a general motivation, but a student of public health wouldn't find it compelling. Different people are motivated by different problems. In reading, then, we can ask: what audience is motivated by the issues chosen by the author?

If we define a problem as an educational issue, then the audience is implicitly defined as people interested in education. If we define the educational issue as "school outcomes," we might refine our audience further, and if we define specific outcomes (e.g., test scores, grades, college acceptance, future earning, etc.), then we further define the audience as those interested in those specific types of outcomes.

Every choice a researcher makes will shape the audience. Choosing a specific method limits the audience to those who support the method. Choosing a specific theoretical premise excludes those who reject the premise. The various choices made shape the audience to whom a work will speak.

Stylistic choices may also influence the audience: certain forms of language speak more to some audiences than others. The notoriously convoluted language commonly associated with post-modern philosophies is itself enough to exclude many, whether that prose is intentionally difficult to shape the audience or simply the outcome of a struggle to express difficult ideas.

Another main factor defining the audience is the use of literature: many people react strongly to specific sources, so using a source can define an audience very effectively. The next section will discuss use of literature in greater depth.

In your practice of deep reading, you can look at a work to see how it speaks to some people and excludes others. Seeing how others approach audiences will provide guidance when you are writing about your own work.

Exercises (5 to 10 minutes, repeat a couple of times)

Pick a specific work. What can you tell about its audience based on its publication information? What does the publisher or the journal tell you about the audience? Is the author famous, and if so, what audience does that author cater to? Does the year of publication influence who the audience might be? How?

Look at the abstract (if there is one), or the opening paragraph. Pick a statement that will limit the audience in some way. What audience is included by that statement and what audience is excluded?

Use of other literature

The literature used in a describing a research project helps define the audience. Readers are more likely to keep reading a work that relies on sources they respect.

For those works that you do choose to read deeply, if you look at the way your readings rely on other academic literature, you can get guidance on how to use literature in your own writing about your own research project. And the more closely the topic of your reading matches your own project, the greater the potential to use the same sources, too.

Reports on specific research results handle literature differently from textbooks and elementary readings. Recognizing the difference between how literature is used to give an overview of a field (as in a textbook) and how literature is used to explain a single study (as in a research article) is extremely valuable when it comes to writing about your own work.

Most of the literature that scholars produce and publish in journals uses the other literature in the field very efficiently. In the vast majority of scholarly works, authors set the context and motivation for their scholarship by using other research literature. When reading scholarly articles, look at the way in which other authors rely on the literature. Who do they use, and how do they use them?

Who is used?
Scholars use citations when defining the premises with which they work. Every author has heroes and/or villains that they identify with the parts of the discourse that matter most.

Scholars mention others scholars to provide comparisons to help define their points, whether to build on some other work or to contradict it. Given that published works dedicate significant effort to defining the ideas that they use, these previous published works can serve as foundations for your own discussion of the same or a similar idea. Authors connect with a whole system of reasoning with a few citations, allowing them to move very quickly to their own novel contribution.

Note that what works for published authors doesn't always work for graduate students, so published work is not a perfect model for your own writing. A professor might treat the same claim and citation differently in different contexts: while acting as a peer reviewer for a journal, with concern for the quality of material published in the journal, they might accept a quick claim and citation in a place where, while acting as a professor concerned with the accreditation of the student, they might desire more explanatory material regarding sources used.

How other literature is used

There is a range of positions we can take with respect to other ideas, so when reading the literature, you can look for the ways in which authors position themselves with respect to others. Most simply, look to see whether authors agree or disagree. But often the use of other material is more nuanced: one author uses another's ideas as a starting position, but modifies the premises in some way. Or, while accepting a basic framework, the author may focus on a specific disagreement within that framework. Or the author may accept all that has gone before to explore a possible extension of the work. When reading, ask, how do other authors use their sources?

Because literature is a reflection of a conversation among scholars, the material cited by an author sets most of the context in which the work can be understood. Returning to the metaphor of reading a specific work as hearing only one side of a telephone conversation, we can think of the literature cited as clues to what is being said on the other end of the line.

Literature as a source of definition

One concern for an academic writer is to define terms carefully and in a way that can be understood. Definition can be problematic for many reasons. Sometimes it can seem necessary to define the terms used in the definition, which is a slippery slope, because each new definition is open to question. Let us say, for example, that we want to define "intelligence" as "being able to use tools." In such a definition, if we want to be precise, we might ask: what is a tool? And what is it to "use" a tool? Is a stick wielded by a primate to draw ants out of an anthill a "tool"? What about the twig with which a bird builds its nest? Or, let us say that we're trying to define "intelligence" as the ability to use language. What is "language"? Are the communicative "dances" of bees "language"?

Attempts at definition often become complicated at boundary cases, as we see in the attempts to define intelligence above. Whatever boundary case we might choose can become associated with some other phenomenon that might or might not be accepted: thus we might or might not choose to consider the materials in a bird's nest to be "tools."

A good way to get around this—one that many authors use—is to draw on the definitions used by other authors. By using someone else's definition—especially one that has been published and used by published literature—you can sidestep the debate. Using a previously published definition allows you to say, "This term is used as it has generally been used in the literature." The subtext of such a statement includes claiming:

> The many debates that have surrounded this term are part of using the definition, and I, the author, understand those limits and concerns, but those debates are not under discussion here. In this work, I will focus on the term as defined.

When reading, look at how authors define their terms. Do they define them? Or which do they define? How often do they use other authors to define terms? Do they use definitions that you would use? What do you think of their definitions? Do they leave some terms undefined that you would expect them to define?

Exercises (30 minutes)

Look in one of your readings for some uses of literature. Are they effective or confusing? Can you engage with literature in your own work in the same way as the reading?

Style and rhetorical models

In the section on attitude, I defended the poor quality of academic writing. I essentially argued that such stylistic concerns are secondary to the intellectual work, and that what really matters are the fundamental premises of research—initial assumptions, questions, hypotheses, methods, and so on—which are independent of the written form, in the sense that any specific premise can be represented in several different but roughly equivalent forms.

If we believe that ideas can be separated from specific linguistic forms—for example, that an idea can be translated from one language to another—then we can see stylistic choices as those that shape the specific presentation of ideas without altering the ideas presented. This is basically what I argued in the section on bad writing when I defended such writing.

Although the stylistic choices made in writing are secondary, such choices have to be made and some mode of presentation must be chosen. When it comes to writing up your own work, I recommend focusing your attention on expressing the ideas, and trying to do that as clearly and simply as possible without explicitly trying to be stylish (which, of course, is a stylistic choice). But when it comes to reading, it can be interesting to focus on the stylistic matters: what makes a work read well? What makes it read poorly? If you think about those issues when you're reading, it can inform your writing practice, too.

When reading, you can look for a few stylistic issues that can be used as models:

1. How is the work introduced? Is there a bald statement of subject to start (e.g., "This article is about XYZ")? Or perhaps there is an example (e.g., some vignette that brings the example to life)? Or is there some context, historical or otherwise (e.g., Kant saying "Ever since Hume ...")? How soon does the author move to the main question? Is it stated in the first paragraph? On the first page?
2. Is material presented in a simple fashion or a complex one? Is that the result of an author's inability to express him/herself clearly, or is it some intentional choice? Is this style a matter of convention in a field (i.e., is this author's writing more or less clear than others writing on the same topic)?
3. Does the author use sentences or phrases that indicate how the immediate focus relates to the larger argument? For example, are there transitional sentences that say "We have just finished talking about subject X, and now we are moving on to subject Y. These relate to the main argument in the following way ..."? Or "The argument that follows will address the following points in order: X, Y, Z ..."?[4]

Some matters of style unrelated to content

Some academic writing is beautifully crafted art. And some academic writing strives to be beautifully crafted without success. Some academic writing tries to be as complex as possible, while other writing struggles to present complex ideas simply. Some authors try to be consciously stylish.

Part of being a scholar is writing, and it can help your writing to be consciously aware of stylistic issues, so, when reading, it may be useful to consider stylistic choices that lie outside purely theoretical ends.

As a reader, consider stylistic differences in the works that you read: what are the models that you want or need to emulate? To the extent that the writing styles used by other writers in your research community define what is acceptable to members of that community, you want to be able to emulate their style. It can be beneficial to be able to "sound" like other scholars in your field. And to some extent, it's natural to develop language like the people you read: if a work influences you, you will naturally tend to copy that language.

Style matters. Every author has a reasonable concern for motivating interest in the reader and engaging style can motivate interest. Content may be what is most important to the scholar, but writing well does matter, because good writing can be the difference between being read and being ignored.[5]

Presentation can take a variety of forms; there is no one right way to write about research. But still, general conventions have arisen—and can be seen in any body of academic literature—and these conventions arose because they helped scholars work together.[6] As you practice reading, give some thought to styles and conventions: what kinds of language and modes of presentation are common in your field?

> **Exercises** (15 minutes)
>
> What is an example of work that is well written but poorly thought out? What are the strengths of the writing? Are they enough to overcome the conceptual weakness (do other people respect the work more than you)?
>
> What is an example of work that is poorly written but well thought out? What are the weaknesses of the writing? Are they enough to obscure the conceptual strengths?

Questions: from concept to practical research

The big questions that motivate us are not always questions for which we can get a direct answer. Many things of interest are not clear or easily defined. The U.S. Supreme Court Justice Potter Stewart famously said that with respect to pornography/obscenity, "I know it when I see it." If you have attained the pinnacle of your profession, you may be able to get away with, "I know it when I see it," but that probably won't satisfy the peer reviewers at a journal, and few professors would accept that from a dissertation writer. Scholars provide definitions of terms so that others can understand their reasoning. But translating general ideas into definitions is difficult. Justice Stewart's declaration about pornography may be satisfactory from the perspective of common sense, but the scholar needs to explain so that other researchers can test the work or build on it. Many concepts are easily understood at the level of common sense, but how can they be defined for research? How can they be observed and measured?

There is a gap between the ideas that are meaningful in everyday life and things that can provide observable data suitable for research. What, for example, is a precise, scholarly definition of intelligence, and how is it measured? The variety of different intelligence tests is clear evidence that researchers do not all agree on how to measure intelligence.

I have earlier argued that defining a research project is itself a difficult task. When you read, you can look at how other authors set up their research questions, and how they moved from the general questions that shaped their overall motivations, to the specific questions that defined their projects.

The step that bridges the gap between theoretical construct (idea) and observable data is known as operationalization, and it's a difficult jump.

In reading, look for how other authors translate the general concepts they want to discuss into a plan for gathering information. How are the more general concepts that may not be directly observable linked to specific things that can be observed?

Research wants objective data; it wants evidence. That is to say, it needs something that can be observed without too much debate about interpretation.[7] This is one reason that numbers are so valued in empirical research: counts and simple measurements are not subject to the worst issues of interpretation. For example, a researcher can directly and object- ively observe and record the specific words in a text—the number of times that Thomas Kuhn used the word "paradigm" in *The Structure of Scientific Revolutions* is not really subject to debate—but a researcher cannot as easily and objectively interpret Kuhn's intentions.

If you want to do work that others will agree with, you have a reason to find observable phenomena to use for data for your analyses of the world, but translating a concept into observable phenomena isn't easy. When you are reading research, you want to look for the ways in which other scholars translate abstract concepts into things that can be observed—both because it helps you analyze their work, and because it helps you design your own.

An example of this process is given by Alan Turing at the beginning of his famous "Computing Machinery and Intelligence" (1950).[8] I previously mentioned the difficulty of defining "intelligence" and noted different observable phenomena that might or might not count as intelligence. Turing begins his article: "I propose to consider the question, 'Can machines think?' This should begin with definitions of the terms 'machine' and 'think'." But he immediately observes the problems coming up with these necessary definitions, and decides to shift his attention: "Instead of attempting such a definition I shall replace the question by another, which is closely related to it and is expressed in relatively unambiguous words."

Turing starts with the general question he wants to ask, but seeing it as an unanswerable question, he tries a different but parallel question that he believes can be answered. That redefinition begins with his dissatisfaction with possible definitions of complex terms, and ends with his creation of what he considers a relatively unambiguous question/test. Instead of the general conceptual question of whether machines can think—"thinking" can't easily be defined, and this can't easily be turned into empirical data—it is replaced with a practical question: can a machine perform a certain task? In this case, a task that has a simple yes/no answer (did the person communicating with the machine think that he/she was communicating with a machine?), eliminating the problems created by the difficulty in defining "think."

This gap from conceptual question to a practical, observable question is crucial in a lot of research. Looking to see how the authors you read make the transition from abstract question to specific research project can help you bridge this gap as you design your own research.

Exercises (10 minutes, repeat as appropriate)

Consider one work you have read. How does it bridge the gap between what the authors want to examine and what they can examine? Or, to take the same point from a slightly different angle: how do the authors decide what kinds of evidence to gather to support their claims?

Reading checklist/questionnaire

This questionnaire tries to cover the variety of questions and issues that are relevant when you read a work. It may not be exhaustive, but the point of working with this list is not to test your knowledge, but rather to give you ideas that might help you use the literature more productively. At any given moment, you might read with only a few of these considerations in mind. As you revisit the most important works (most important to you), you will likely be focusing on different issues at different times, and comprehensive coverage of the issues in this questionnaire might only come after a few readings.

Source

1. Who is the author and what are the author's institutional affiliations?
2. Who is the publisher? Is it a popular source or an academic one?

Type of article/Audience

1. What kind of work is this? Popular or academic? Empirical or theoretical?
2. Who is the intended audience for this work?

Definitions

1. What are the terms they define?
2. How do these definitions compare to other definitions of the same terms found in other literature?
3. How do these definitions compare to your understanding of the subject? (As always, be willing to challenge the published literature.)

Evidence

1. What sorts of evidence are presented? Empirical? Logical/rational? Other?
2. What sorts of data are presented?

Quality

1. Rate the overall quality of the work

   - Is the argument sound?
   - Is the evidence sound?
   - Are the methods appropriate?
   - Is the writing clear?

Motivation

1. What motivations are provided for the research?

   a. What motivations explain the choice of subject?
   b. What motivations explain the choice of method?

Methods

1. What data gathering techniques are being used?
2. What analytical methods are being used?

3. Are the data gathering techniques suitable for the analytical methods? Why or why not?[9]

Models

1. What models used in this article could you copy in your own work?

   - Methods?
   - Motivations?
   - Rhetorical devices?
   - Sources?

Heroes and villains/Use of literature

1. Who are the sources that the author considers allies/supporters?
2. Who are the sources the author considers enemies?
3. Would you consider the author to be an ally or enemy?

Overall review

1. Do you agree or disagree with the work?

   a. What specific points do you agree with?
   b. What specific points do you disagree with?

2. Can you use the work to develop your own work? How?

Project 5: deep reading

Pick one work that you have already read and that you think might be valuable for your research. I recommend picking an article or single chapter in a book rather than an entire book, just to keep the piece you analyze smaller.

Part 1: Deep reading

1. What kind of research did they do, and could you emulate it? Could you do a project similar to theirs (but not identical)?
2. Why did they do that research? What were their motivations? What was the large problem that frames the work? What are the more precise motivations that led to the specific focus of the work?

3. Who was their audience? Or, who are different audiences that might be interested in parts of their work?
4. Use of other literature: how do they use it? What kinds of literature do they use? How much of their space do they spend writing about other literature?
5. Who is(are) the author(s)? Have they done other pertinent works? Are they a big name in the field?
6. How is their writing? Is it effective? How do they deal with the weaknesses of their work?
7. How do they frame their general question?
8. How do they move from general question to specific research project?

Part 2: Process analysis

1. How long did you spend reading that single work?
2. Was the effort worth it?
3. Can you spend an equal amount of time on everything you read? Or do you have to limit the amount of time you spend on some works? (OK, so I know that I have repeatedly suggested that you can't, but do you agree? Why or why not?)

Notes

1 Obviously, you don't want to get lost reading, but realistically, the academic literature is complicated and difficult and still worth the effort.
2 Replication studies—attempts to copy the research methods and recreate the results—are often desirable, but not trivial to execute.
3 Of course, there are ways that a researcher in education could express a concern for a pathology X, like studying the impact of pathology X on school performance, or by developing programs for students with pathology X.
4 I call remarks like these "signposts" for their role in helping the reader orient themselves in the larger landscape of ideas, and get a sense of the direction of the narrative.
5 In his "Apologie for Poetrie," Sir Philip Sidney argues that the poet is a better teacher than the philosopher because the poet is more likely to engage the reader: "For suppose it be granted—that which I suppose with great reason may be denied—that the philosopher, in respect of his methodical proceeding, teach more perfectly than the poet, yet do I think that no man is so much [a lover of philosophy—'philo-philosophos'] as to compare the philosopher in moving with the poet. And that moving is of

a higher degree than teaching, it may by this appear, that it is well nigh both the cause and the effect of teaching; for who will be taught, if he be not moved with desire to be taught?" From Project Gutenberg: www.gutenberg.org/files/1962/1962-h/1962-h.htm.

6 At least some conventions are developed to help scholars work together. The conventions of style manuals on formatting and such are aimed at making works easier to read. Conventions for referencing works, in particular, are intended to help a reader more easily discern the nature of the work being cited. They may be a nuisance for a writer, but they're not just arbitrary restrictions.

7 In literary criticism, the words of a text being examined are relatively objective, at least in the sense that different scholars agree on which set of words are being interpreted. Different scholars may differ on how to interpret, for example, Hamlet's monologue, but they (usually) agree that it begins, "To be or not to be."

8 Turing, A. M. "Computing Machinery and Intelligence." *Mind, Volume LIX*, Issue 236, October 1950, pages 433–460, https://doi.org/10.1093/mind/LIX.236.433

9 In general, published work will have a pretty good match between analysis and data gathering—it is certainly to be hoped that peer reviewers working for journals or publishers would check this. But peer review systems are fallible and subject to abuse. Not all work that is accepted and published meets this basic criterion.

Writing about literature

The process of research design often produces a piece of writing that is called a "literature review." The question for the two final chapters is, "how do you write a literature review?" Part of the answer, of course, is "practice," but we can add some detail to that.

Throughout the book, I have been arguing that the academic literature is a conversation. When you're reading, you're listening to what others have to say. Writing is your chance to share your own voice and vision. It is your chance for others to listen to you. And that has its advantages and disadvantages.

Earlier, I stressed the importance of confidence for reading, but for writing, confidence is even more crucial. Silent listening invites no reproach, but handing in a written work to your professors? That invites a response. Professors are supposed to critique, of course, but even so, even thinking that you will receive supportive and constructive feedback, it's still hard to receive feedback. This, speaking simplistically, is the reason that people get writer's block, not reader's block: it's the written work that gets the critique.

Remaining silent won't do if you need to write a dissertation. Writing is your necessary entry into the scholarly conversation, starting with your project proposal, which you introduce into your immediate research community, starting with your professors. When you enter that conversation, you can start by telling your readers about the voices to whom you are responding: who are the heroes and villains who have inspired and guided you on your quest for knowledge? That is part of the story that you will tell.

When you're writing about your project—whether a proposal, or the final draft—you're pretty much expected to write about the literature, whether or not you have to write something titled "literature review." If you have developed your project in conjunction with the literature—if you have taken ideas or models from the literature and woven them into your own research story— then this is hardly any added burden, because it's already part of what you're doing, not some added extraneous task. If you developed your research using a theory—for example, W.E.B. Du Bois's theory of double consciousness or Geertz's idea of "thick description"—then you have a choice in writing: do you write a full description of that theory or do you just write "Du Bois's double consciousness" or "Geertz's thick description"? Obviously, if you can count on your audience understanding the reference, it's easier to just refer to the theory than it is to describe it.

At all times, your research must reflect your own vision; but, assuming your vision has been influenced by what you read or heard from others, then you can use the literature to help explain yourself. A comparison between your vision and some piece of published literature gives your readers context that helps them understand your work.

To write about the literature well takes practice. Writing is difficult. Trying to fit into the scholarly conversation is difficult. There is no "right" answer in how to write about your work, though there are plenty of useful conventions that you can follow, if they suit your purposes. With practice and the willingness to write, get it wrong, and write it again, you can develop the ability to produce documents that help you—not just the dissertation as a whole, but the whole correspondence that goes with any research, including administrative materials, etc.

The first chapter of Part 3 (Chapter 6) is concerned with the practice of writing and especially the practice of writing about literature. It parallels many of the concerns of reading, starting with the importance of developing your own vision and voice, and including ideas like engaging in conversation with your heroes and villains, and also discusses some general issues of writing practice.

The second (Chapter 7) focuses on "literature reviews"—the different kinds of projects/written works that are called a "literature review,"—and more specifically on writing the literature review section of a dissertation (traditionally, the second chapter of many dissertations, particularly in the social sciences).

Writing with literature

As mentioned in the chapter on research practice (Chapter 2), writing is a skill that develops with practice, as is writing about the literature.

During the process of research and research design, writing is a valuable tool on many levels, from record keeping to exploration of ideas to sharing your ideas with others. Working on writing in any of these capacities will help you develop general skill as a writer: the more you practice putting your ideas into words on the page, the better you get. Practice won't necessarily make the task easier—writing is hard!—but it will help you get more out of your efforts. To return to the cooking metaphor, an experienced chef might work just as hard as a novice, but the chef would produce the better meal.

If you are developing a research practice approach, as I have been suggesting, then your relationship to the literature will be developing alongside your own ideas and your own research project. This chapter discusses a number of considerations with regard to the practice of writing about literature that you can apply in your own writing practice. Some of these considerations relate to developing a practice; others are more specific suggestions for putting your ideas into words.

Part of your job as an independent researcher is convincing your readers that you did your job well.[1] Whether you are a student or an established scholar, you need to convince the gatekeepers (professors, editors, peer reviewers, grant reviewers) that your work is worthy. In the abstract, this means satisfying the general standards expected in your field. In practice, this means meeting the expectations of a few people.

When writing, your explanations are delivered to a specific audience with specific interests and expectations. If you want to convince that audience, it helps to write their language. If you think and write about your research as if you were engaging in conversation with previous researchers (who speak through their publications), you will tend to adopt the right language as a product of responding to their concerns.

Use the literature as a tool; don't tolerate it as an imposed requirement

Use literature because it helps you tell your own story. Write about literature to provide comparison to your own work and ideas. This is directly parallel to the attitude needed for reading: you engage the literature because it helps you do what you want to do, because it helps you achieve some purpose of your own, or answer some question that you have.

If you're a doctoral candidate, there is certainly a significant expectation that you are familiar with the larger body of literature in your field. But is that what a dissertation or dissertation proposal is supposed to show? When you're writing your dissertation, is the task to design and complete a research project, or to prove that you've read enough? To complete your own research project, you need to stay focused on the specific purpose of your research, and on the literature that led you to that purpose.

In the section on reading literature, I argued for seeing how the literature relates to your own vision of the world and your own project, and for considering how sources in the literature share or contrast with your own ideas. If you start to see your own ideas as related to ideas in the published literature, then the literature is a tool to explain what you think, not some extra burden to carry for the sake of form.

Write with purpose

Writing grows from a purpose, and purposes are context-sensitive. Good writing in one context is not good writing in another. The better your sense of purpose for each specific thing that you write, the easier it is to accomplish your goals, and to know how much and what literature to write about. You don't just want to say whatever people expect you to say—that leads to problems when you want to express your own voice—but you do want to try to understand what they want and expect. From content, to focus, to length and language; what you put on the page is shaped by the context in which it will be read.

The better you can keep your purposes in view, the better you can write in a way that suits the audience. But purposes are complex and multi-layered.

One layer of purposes are those concerning what a written work accomplishes or helps you accomplish. Are you writing for yourself? Is it to explore? Is it to keep records? Or are you writing to someone else? If you are writing to someone else, what do you want their response to be? Are you writing something to get feedback? Or are you writing something to get it accepted? A clear sense of what you want to accomplish helps focus your efforts and your writing. If you're just making exploratory notes for yourself, you can do anything without worrying about legibility; if you're making records for yourself, they need to be sufficiently legible for you to use in the future; if you're looking for feedback on an early draft, it's important to proofread, but not to be error-free; if you're submitting a final draft that will go into your university library, you'd like to be error-free. Those different contexts call for different amounts of effort spent working on the language.

At another layer, we can see different purposes for different parts of a written work. This is, perhaps, obvious: an introduction introduces a work, a methods section describes methods used, etc.—the different parts of a work each have a specific purpose. Seeing these purposes helps you organize your work. Viewed in this light, an outline for your discussion grows out of a sense of purpose rather than a sense of convention. In light of these different purposes, the progression from introduction to literature review to methods can be seen as a tool to draw others in and convince them of your work's value: first you give a general description so your audience knows what you're talking about and so they have reasons to care enough to keep reading (introduction). Next, you give details about the important ideas that influenced you (literature review), and then you describe how you're putting those ideas into action (methods). Seeing each section as serving a specific purpose provides some guidance for each section.

And at yet another layer, there are different purposes with respect to the intellectual/theoretical dimensions of your work. You may wish to promote some ideas and build on them. At other times, you may want to correct something that seems a misconception to you. Theoretical purposes go a long way toward motivating your choice of what literature to write about: if you have some theory that you want to discuss, then you have a reason to discuss literature related to that theory.

Writing for practice vs. writing for product

If you want to build a good practice, it's important to be able to write for practice sometimes, and at other times to write with an eye toward producing a finished work. Writing to produce finished work is necessarily fraught with all the anxieties of receiving feedback, which is why it is so valuable to write for practice. It's difficult to clearly explain stuff in writing—it's difficult to explain theories (yours and others'); it's difficult to explain methods; it's difficult to explain observations. Telling your own story is hard, and harder if you're still trying to figure out your own story. Those difficulties are compounded if you're also concerned with getting your grammar right, and making sure you punctuated correctly. If you write for practice, you don't have to concern yourself with getting everything perfect, and you can focus on getting your words out.

Think of the difference between speech and writing: most people can speak about their ideas coherently and rapidly, showing that they can think about their ideas coherently and rapidly. Why can you not write just as rapidly? OK, there are mechanical differences: typing is slower than speech. But other than that, what stops you from writing just as quickly as you speak? With practice, it becomes possible to write more quickly, especially if you stop worrying about grammar. Setting aside concern for grammar while writing for practice can indirectly improve grammar in the long run. If you get better at getting your ideas onto the page in a quick (if messy) form, you have more time to spend editing and proofreading, which allows you to improve the quality of your written product, and actually allows you more time to think about grammatical issues, which will improve your grammar.

Grammar and punctuation play a valuable role in helping express meaning, so I do not want to discount their importance. Grammar and punctuation are tools for helping you develop your own ideas and tools for helping you communicate with others, so in the long run you want to get them right. But for researchers struggling to develop a writing practice, grammar can add a level of difficulty. First learn to get your ideas onto the page in a rough form; then learn to do that in more elegant forms, and with greater efficiency.

With practice, your "messy" early drafts are better and have fewer errors, and each writing task can be accomplished with greater confidence. Write for practice as much as possible. Write for product only when it's time to turn something in. With practice, these two purposes can start to merge in the sense that you can worry about writing well at the same time as you struggle with expression. As skill grows, there is less to be done when it's time to turn an early exploratory draft into a draft that you share with others.

Exercises (10 minutes)

When do you write? What are your purposes when you write? Do you write to turn in material? Do you write notes for brainstorming? For personal records? Do you write correspondence with professors or fellow students? What are some of the different things you have written about your research, to whom have you written those things, and what was your purpose in writing? How do these different purposes shape what you write?

Drafts and feedback

As a general matter, it's good to get feedback on your work when navigating the difficult territory of research design, especially if you're uncertain of your direction. And when you're writing about literature, it's hard to anticipate exactly what your readers are going to expect of you, and thus easy to write too much. Sending off drafts and getting feedback can help you identify the limits of how much written review of literature is necessary, in addition to helping you work out any theoretical issues you might have in developing your research project.

Write drafts quickly and write several. And, at suitable times, share those drafts and ask for feedback. You may think that I'm very casual about writing many drafts quickly, but if you practice writing quickly, that becomes less of an issue. Again, think about how quickly you can speak. If you can write a draft that captures your train of thought quickly, then writing multiple drafts is not such a burden. Most students have written quickly at times—during exams, producing papers at the last minute—so the ability is there. With practice, that writing speed can be harnessed early in the process rather than only at the last minute.

Practically speaking, if you finish a work quickly, you may sacrifice quality in the short run, but finishing quickly leaves time for your readers to give you feedback, and gives you time to respond to it. In the long run, this process will help improve the quality of your work. And though you may have to push to finish a draft quickly, that early push can help you avoid the stress of looming deadlines.

By completing a draft, you yourself can see the whole project in a new light, and this can be instructive enough to guide you to a new draft. If you write one draft quickly, then you will feel less concern about writing a next draft, and you will also have more time to write that new draft.

Further, if you share a draft with someone, there's a good chance you'll learn something useful. Perhaps your reader will give you some wonderful feedback that helps you refine your work. Perhaps your reader will completely miss the point. You can learn from both.

As in so many parts of practice, there is a balance to be found here. You want to send off drafts to get feedback, but you don't want to send so many drafts that your readers start to tune you out. Generally, it's good to set a schedule with your readers: what schedule would your professors like you to keep? Do they want you to send them some writing each month? Or each term? It's worth a conversation to find out what their expectations are with respect to schedules. And then it's worth the effort to keep that schedule, including the difficult task of turning in a work that is still problematic to make a deadline.

Getting feedback is difficult, and it requires confidence. But it can get easier with practice—partly, you get used to people criticizing your work, and, perhaps more importantly, you get used to sorting the useful points from the less useful. This is especially true if you feel the confidence to respond to feedback as part of your conversation with scholars in your field.

It doesn't feel good to have someone write nasty things about your work, but not all feedback is equally good. Professors make mistakes. They don't always give good feedback—good in the sense of constructive and supportive, good in the sense of being courteous, or even good in the sense of accurate and on target. I've seen professors misunderstand what their students have written on many occasions. For that matter, I've misunderstood what someone wrote and later gone back and wondered how I ever came to such a flawed interpretation.

Take a critical and analytic eye to feedback, just as you would to the literature you read: which parts are useful and which aren't? Where is the reviewer on target and where did they miss? Which parts can you put into your work, and which do you ignore? Feedback is only one first response to your voice entering the scholarly conversation; try to use it to move forward and develop your work.

A few suggestions for receiving feedback:

1. Separate the comments on your writing (grammar, spelling, style, etc.) from the comments on your ideas.
2. Separate the issues that are easy to fix from the ones that aren't.
3. Prioritize comments that are on your ideas, and then comments that are easy to fix.

Exercises (5–10 minutes)

How well do you deal with feedback?

How often do you think that the feedback you get is useful and constructive?

How often do you think that the feedback you get is negative or destructive?

Target lengths

One of the great dangers in writing about research literature is that there is so much to write about.[2] Just as there is danger in the reader saying, "I need to read one more article," it's deceptively easy for a writer to get bogged down in a cycle of saying, "I need to mention just one more author." Target lengths help prevent unnecessary expansion. Target lengths are generally useful for a writer, so, as with the previous section, this is not strictly a matter of writing about literature, but it is advice that is particularly valuable because there is so much literature that could be included in a written work.

My opinion on target lengths has changed over time. When I was younger, I would have said it was bad to focus on the length, and that one should, instead, focus on what "needs to be said." Length, I would have argued, is determined by content, and not vice versa. Focusing on length, I thought, would lead to padding pages with useless material.

Now, with greater experience, I think that target lengths are very useful for avoiding the big pitfall of writing too much. As for the question of what "needs to be said": set limits on the basis of practical considerations because they cannot be set using only theoretical concerns.

Setting a target is a reasonable attempt to suit your work to the context in which it will be presented. What is appropriate to your context? Think about your audience and how to get them to respond favorably to your own work. If you are given an explicit limit of 500 words (in an IRB proposal or grant/fellowship application, for example), will you benefit from writing 1,000 words? If your professors expect twenty pages, will they be happy if you give them fifty? Extra words or pages do not help get a work accepted, especially if they take you over a length limit. They don't help you, and they take additional time to write and edit, which is a bad allocation of effort.

You want to know what your audience expects, so that you can give them something close to what they want. I suggest setting a target somewhat below the expectation, perhaps 60% to 75%, for a few reasons. Firstly, shorter drafts are less difficult to write and also less intimidating. What's easier to write, a ten-page paper or a twenty-page paper? Practically speaking, saving time is good, and any reduction in stress is an added benefit.

Secondly, if your target is 75% of the expected length, it gives you space to exceed your target without exceeding your readers' desires. In my experience, this is crucial because scholars usually have plenty to say. The common problem for writers, as I have already argued, is trying to say too much.[3]

If you are deep into the details of your work, and are generally familiar with the different published positions on issues related to your work, it can be very easy to slip into lengthy discussion of literature on a given point. Such discussion can take your attention away from your own research. Target lengths prevent this uncontrolled exploration and force you to focus on the most central pieces.

Exercises (5 minutes)

Do you write too much or too little?

What's the longest paper you've ever written? Was it too long, too short, or just right? Was it difficult to write? Would it be intimidating to write a paper that long again? What about a paper twice that long?

Is there any length of paper that you do feel confident writing?

Focal, contextual, and tangential materials

Setting a target length, as discussed in the previous section, is a method to help avoid the danger of spending too much effort writing about material that is not absolutely central to your own research.

I often work with writers who get bogged down in matters that are logically related to their own concerns, but that don't forward their own project. Generally, this happens when they get wrapped up in details of an issue that is important for their work, but only as a challenge to what is foundational to their work. It's important to be able to build on foundations without getting lost looking at the details of those foundations.

This can take some different forms.

One way is to get lost discussing context. Authors can be interested in addressing a problem, and then spend their time describing the problem without moving on to how to address the problem. The problem may be central to everything they do, but extensive detailed description of that problem can lead to many tangential concerns.

For example, a public health researcher examining public policies aimed at drug abuse might get lost in discussing the problem of drug abuse—there are mountains of research that document negative effects of drug use/abuse at both personal and societal levels. That material is contextually important to any study on drug abuse, but, depending on specific focus, very little description may be necessary. Suppose the researcher is studying the effects of government policies to deter drug abuse? How much discussion of the negative effects of drug abuse is necessary, then? Do we need five pages? Or would it suffice to simply say, "we've got a problem, and lots of people have been writing policies to combat it."? If the plan is to examine the impact of different policies, you absolutely have to write about the policies, which will be a massive project in itself. In that case, how much discussion of the problem of drug abuse is necessary to set the context?

Or, for example, an educator might be interested in some pedagogy to address problems in an educational system (e.g., poor outcomes for some group). For that educator, writing extensively about the nature of the problem—what outcomes were measured, where, when, and how—could be an extensive discussion. But how much is necessary before entering into the also extensive discussion of different pedagogical theories, which is much more focal?

Generally, if you are addressing some problem, it's pretty easy to get lost discussing details of the problem, even if those details don't directly relate to your own work. While those details are important in the larger context of your research, they are not all focal to your work. If your entire work is motivated by an attempt to deal with some problem, the problem deserves *some* general discussion because it's important to set the broad context for your work; but detailed examination should be limited to the specific details of your approach that make it different from other related research.

Another way to write too much is to discuss theoretical debates that you are not personally examining. Broad theoretical battles should be left outside any specific research project that is not specifically focused on that battle. If you're studying psychotherapy, for example, don't waste your effort debating the difference between different therapeutic theories. State your foundations and move on from there. Basic theoretical concerns must receive some discussion because you want your reader to understand your work. But you don't want to have to debate your foundations. If you use some controversial idea or author, you may have to acknowledge the controversy, but you don't have to fight the battle. If one of your heroes is controversial, you don't have to fight her/his battles if your work is trying to build on their foundation.

Perhaps the worst case I ever saw of misplaced effort was an author who was interested in pedagogy at evangelical Christian colleges. Her interest, as stated by her abstract and introduction, was in applying a specific pedagogical model at these schools. Her dissertation draft, when I saw it, was maybe 60,000 words, and the vast majority was dedicated to the debate about whether or not evangelical Christian colleges should exist. There was little discussion of pedagogical theory, and almost none on the specific model of interest or the study that she wanted to carry out. She had written a book on whether evangelical Christian colleges should exist, but her research was only meaningful if such colleges do exist. Given that it was a foundation that she was not going to debate, she could have passed over that larger debate in a page or even a sentence: "While it is important to acknowledge the debate about these colleges, this project believes in their value and focuses on specific pedagogical practices suitable for them."

Don't get stuck in big debates![4] Focus on your own specific project and its questions, and on the literature that supports your work. It's important to touch on potential weaknesses of your foundations, but such discussion should not keep you from discussing what you want to do.

Another danger is excessive definition of crucial terminology. Scholarship is supposed to define its terms, but this means that every author defines terms, creating significant variety in definitions for a single term. If your work all depends on one specific definition of a specific term from a published author, then you don't want to spend time and effort getting deep in discussion of the other definitions; you want to rely on the authority of the source you have chosen as a foundation.

Target lengths are very useful in constraining discussion of contextual material and tangential debates. The shorter you set your targets, the greater the need to exclude materials, which forces a choice in favor of the focal materials.

Exercises (10 minutes)

What is the focal matter of your research? What are contextual issues or theoretical controversies that could lead you into extensive discussions that take you away from your focal issues? Are there any problems (e.g., drug abuse, poor student outcomes) that you could address at length and that would take you away from your own research? What about controversies relating to theories that you are using?

Situating your work

You want to give your reader a sense of the discourse in your research community and how your research fits into it without getting sucked into extensive tangential debate. This section discusses some rhetorical techniques for managing those limits.

Asserting limits

The previous sections were concerned with limiting the amount that you write. You want your audience to accept the limits that you chose as reasonable. To a large extent, this is accomplished simply by asserting that you chose to set a limit. If you assert limits, your audience often will accept that assertion.

One of the most useful lines for an academic writer is, "but that is outside the scope of this work." Telling your reader you have made a choice to stop discussing a certain point implies that you know more than you're saying and thus heads off imputations of ignorance. It can help you stay on your chosen focus rather than getting drawn into debates or digressions. This is another case where you can always add material later, if requested.

Ideas vs. people

One way to avoid getting trapped listing many different people with their various theories is to focus your discussion of literature on specific ideas, not on specific authors. Focusing on a single idea allows you to show awareness of the wider discourse quickly and focus on the work most important to you. You can write, for example, "This discussion focuses on the work of AuthorA and AuthorB, although many others also discussed it (AuthorC; AuthorD; etc.)."

Most ideas—even if originally propounded by a single person—will be expressed by several people, so focusing on ideas reduces the number of different specific works that need to be discussed, while still giving the reader a sense of the larger debate into which your work fits.

Focusing on ideas can also be useful in avoiding emotional reactions associated with some scholars. Some scholars inspire strong emotional responses—Marx and Freud, for example. If you have a reader who will have a strong emotional reaction to some specific scholar that you use, avoid naming that scholar if possible! Focus on the specific idea that they use, and thereby avoid triggering the emotional response. In the case of Freud, for example, many of his theories are still useful (e.g., the unconscious), at the same time as others are discredited (e.g., penis envy). Talking about Freud the person will trigger different associations than talking about "the unconscious." And there are plenty of sources other than Freud that can be cited for a discussion of that idea.

Situating a work: an example

Scholars often assert the dimensions and scope of their discussion with broad claims that they don't even try to support. They begin their work with these broad claims about the literature and don't even get into specific cases until they have gotten past the basic limits they have set. Here is an example from economics: "As with those attempting to explain religious phenomena, economists analyzing the 'miracle' of East Asia's growth tend to fall into two camps–fundamentalists and mystics."[5]

In a sentence, the author encompasses and classifies a whole body of literature ("economists ... fall into two camps"). Two groups are named explicitly as defining the relevant body of literature, and this classification indicates the direction of the coming discussion: a separation between two schools of thought and their various explanations for the economic phenomena observed. It is easy, I think, to pass over this as introductory fluff—there's no heavy theory here—but as a writer, this kind of sentence is effective in moving through the large, general context (where there is a big danger of getting sucked into lengthy tangential discussions) toward the point of focus. Generalizations like this keep you from getting sucked into lengthy digressions when you write.

Using broad generalizations like this is a good way to start presenting ideas to readers. While the generalization may be imperfect, it gives the reader context. A particularly critical reader who is also knowledgeable might have his/her own analysis, and think your generalization is mistaken, but it's unlikely that such a difference in perspective would cause that reader to throw aside the work in disgust. Meanwhile, the less knowledgeable reader can be drawn in with the loose and easily understood generalization, and greater detail and analysis can come later in the text.

There are problems with generalizations, of course, but if you don't use them to set context, you get sucked into details that keep you from your own work. In this case, by asserting a basic two-part scheme, the author is able to keep the discussion from running into all the subtle variations in the literature, while also giving some sense of the broad field of ideas published on the subject.

It should also be noted how this example implicitly defines a third group of scholars: when he mentions "economists analyzing the 'miracle'," he implicitly defines another class of economists: those who are not analyzing the miracle, including, perhaps a group of scholars who study the same history but who have reasons to think it's not a miracle at all. This choice of focus could exclude from discussion scholars with relevant material—there may be, for example, economists studying East Asian economies who have not entered the discourse on the miracle—but the author, quite reasonably, doesn't go there.

You absolutely want to define your concerns, and give a general context to your work; but you want to do so broadly and quickly so that you get into the details of your own work.

Phrases that assert limits on discussion are necessary for scholars, even if they set aside concerns and questions that many would feel important. We can denigrate such phrases as "rhetorical devices," used to ignore valuable material, but you can't write everything. Setting a limit is not an attempt to deceive by ignoring something. Such general statements are not an attempt to argue theoretical points, they are an attempt to situate your own work in the conversation. That means identifying, generally, the groups with whom you are hoping to converse, and writing something that appeals to them. If, as in this example, the goal is to talk about the "Economic Miracle," then the work is properly situated with respect to those scholars talking about the miracle, and does not attempt the more frustrating task of debating with those who doubt that it is a miracle at all.

By situating your work with respect to a group of scholars who share a debate (in this example, those who study the "miracle"), you identify the community with whom you wish to converse, and you get to take for granted those ideas that the community also takes for granted. Earlier, I mentioned a student who had written an excessive literature review on whether evangelical Christian colleges should exist, which was a discussion that situated her work with respect to a community that was debating the existence of such colleges. Instead, if she had situated her work with respect to a group of scholars who all agreed on the value of such colleges, she could have focused on the specific pedagogical issues that were important to her, and would also be important to her audience.

Exercises (15 to 20 minutes)

What are some different fields of knowledge that interest you?

What are some fields of knowledge to which you would like to contribute? Consider describing broad fields (e.g., entire university departments) and more specific fields (e.g., specific working groups, specific journals, specific authors).

What are some fields of knowledge that would be interested in your specific project?

Are there any fields of knowledge that you are not interested in and would not use in your project, but that others might think you ought to include (e.g., your professor wants you to refer to Freudian literature, but you don't think it's a good fit)?

In conversation with heroes and villains

In the section on reading, I said that it's a useful overstatement to speak of heroes and villains, in that positioning your work with respect to specific heroes and villains is valuable in helping your reader understand how you relate to the larger field of literature. If writing is a conversation with other scholars, then the heroes and villains are those with whom we agree and disagree, respectively.

The previous section talked about situating your work with respect to large groups of scholars and broad ideas. But another effective way to set context for your work is to talk about your heroes/models and villains/ foils. In the previous section, I talked about how generalizations are useful in moving quickly past tangential material to the core of your work. Once you're talking about the core of your work, generalizations are less effective and it can be better to get into specific conversation with individuals.

Choosing a single figure to serve as a focus can help with managing a wide variety of related positions. To try to define a group as a whole—for example, "deconstructionists" or "pragmatists," or any other named school of thought—can prove difficult because it's tempting to try to make a generalization that will fit all members and then defend or discuss cases that don't quite fit the definition. That can become a lengthy and mostly fruitless process that takes you away from writing about your own work.[6]

If you choose a single individual to focus on—or better, a specific set of premises that the individual uses—you can write about how their ideas compare with your own. You can focus on a specific idea (or set of ideas) that you are using, or you can focus on a specific idea (or set of ideas) that you want to reject or modify. Both choices allow you to write with a good focus, while also giving your reader a sense of how your work relates to a wider discourse.

When you choose a single author for a focal point, it is useful to introduce that author as an imperfect representative of a larger group. You can acknowledge that variation in the larger group exists to let the reader know that you're not ignoring or ignorant of variations. Then, when you choose to focus on the single focal point, it can be presented as a choice that you have made, rather than as a limit created by the fact that you didn't do work (i.e., the difference between saying or implying, "I read that stuff and I'm choosing not to talk about it," and saying, "I can't talk about that stuff because I haven't read it").

You can say something like:

"In this work, we will use the concept of X as defined by AuthorA."

A construction like this is very efficient in that it implicitly incorporates a whole discourse. This is the kind of construction to use if space is limited. In a doctoral dissertation or master's thesis, the context means that you are more likely to be questioned on the alternatives. Professors often want students to demonstrate their knowledge of the wider field. So if you go on to discuss that single point without discussing alternatives at all, you may invite a question about alternatives, and you don't want to get sucked down a discursive rabbit hole. In such situations, you can add just a couple of sentences that mention other sources without needing to analyze them:

> In this work, we use the concept of X as defined by AuthorA. We recognize that this definition is not universally accepted (see, for example, AuthorB, AuthorC), and in particular we acknowledge the critique of AuthorA's definition offered by AuthorD. Nonetheless, for the purposes of this research, which is not affected by AuthorD's concern, we still adhere to AuthorA in preference to AuthorB and AuthorC. A full discussion of concerns expressed with AuthorA's definition is outside the scope of this work.[7]

Context will determine which version is better, with overall length limits being the main factor. But other concerns of your audience also matter. For example, if you can assume that your audience will be familiar with the debate in question, then you might use a shorter discussion than needed for a less familiar audience. Whichever context, it's good to focus on your main heroes and villains and to leave out the tangential voices.

Focus on main authors is pragmatically effective in controlling the discussion so that you can attend to your main points and main theories. This structure lets you address alternative theories as briefly as possible without sacrificing a focus on your own work. It also allows expansion to larger sizes, if more discussion is needed:

> In this work, we use the concept of X as defined by AuthorA. We recognize that this definition is not universally accepted (see, for example, AuthorB, AuthorC), and in the following paragraphs we will discuss a few important alternatives.
>
> AuthorB has proposed ... , which is similar to points of AuthorC and AuthorD.
>
> AuthorE has proposed ...
>
> A full discussion of all the merits of these various points of view is outside the scope of this work, and so we will return our focus to how concept X (as defined by AuthorA) influences this study of StudyTopic.

As much as possible, try to control the flow of the discourse by keeping your focus on the main focal points of your work, especially the main scholars who shaped your ideas.

Exercises (15 to 20 minutes)

Who are your heroes? Who are your villains? What do you like and/or dislike about them? Do the heroes have bad points and the villains good points?

Which of the heroes and villains will be most useful when trying to write about your own work?

Which of the heroes and villains will be least useful?

Audience

Writing for an audience can be intimidating—it's easy to start thinking about negative feedback you have previously received. If you're just writing notes or exercises, you can make a mess with few repercussions. When writing for an audience, however, there is a real concern for how they will respond, which can create pressure. But writing with an audience in mind can provide useful guidance, too.

If you have a specific audience in mind, you can ask crucial questions: What does your audience need to know? What material do they already know? What can you leave out because they know it? What should you leave out because they might object to it? What language do they speak, and what language do you want to use that might be unfamiliar to your audience?

The same material needs to be presented differently to different people in different contexts. By thinking about your audience and their needs, you can better define the needs of your writing.

Think about the vast difference between describing a theory to 1) a ten-year-old, 2) a college freshman in an introductory class, 3) a college senior in the field, and 4) a doctoral candidate in your field. Each of these audiences will respond effectively to different language and level of detail. Not only do different audiences have different knowledge and language, they also have different motivations. What interests one person doesn't necessarily interest another.

You might consider a number of different factors with respect to your audience.

Knowledge

One obvious concern is the knowledge of your audience. Scholars specialize and often have deep knowledge on one subject but not on others. If you are speaking with the author of a specific article, you can assume that she or he knows the article well. If you are speaking with a different scholar in the field, you may not be able to make the same assumption. Scholars familiar with one school of thought may not be familiar with the fine details of other theories.

An economist with Marxist interests, for example, may not be familiar with details of specific debates among market economists, and vice versa.

When you're a student writing for specific professors (as, for example, a dissertation writer in a U.S. university), then you can have fairly detailed knowledge of your audience. This can be intimidating in some ways, but it can also be helpful in deciding what will convince them.

If you're writing for an uncertain audience—the peer reviewers at a journal, or, in U.K.-style doctoral programs, the professors who will review a dissertation or thesis—you know less, but you can still try to glean useful information about what they might know. For example, you can assume that the peer reviewers at a journal will have some familiarity with the journal's content. For thesis reviewers, you may not know exactly which professors will review your work, but you can certainly get a sense of the different professors in your program. What are the shared interests and knowledge of these potential reviewers? The professors in a program are not a homogeneous group, and it's easy to focus on the differences between professors you know well, which means you can lose sight of larger similarities among them.

Motivation

Another aspect of concern is motivating the reader's interest. Not surprisingly, you will get a better response if your reader cares positively about what you're doing. There are two dimensions to this: first, appealing to the present interests of your readers, and second, creating new interests in your reader. For this task, I think in terms of selling the work, selling the ideas, and selling the research: what will make your reader want the information and ideas that you are sharing? Understanding what the audience wants allows either a direct appeal to their current interests or an indirect appeal by linking your interest to something they already want.

Discussion of why you care and why others should care should be prominent and supported by discussion of publications that also care. Although research is supposed to be objective, the choices of what to research never are: research design starts with the personal interests and knowledge that have guided you to the specific program in which you study.

It can be useful to discuss personal motivations—e.g., "I came to this project because of my experience with ..."—but take care that the discussion doesn't become too personal (and also be aware that some readers will dislike much use of the first person). Thinking about how your interests parallel those of others can guard against becoming too personal: what does your audience care about that you also care about? The greater the overlap between your interests and your readers' interests, the more effective first-person discussion can be. This is, I think, why advertising often employs (allegedly) real customers rather than actors: the "real customer" is supposed to be more relatable.

Discussing your personal interests can lend a passion and authenticity to your voice. But passion and authenticity can interfere, too: you don't want some passion to lead you down a tangent.

Knowing what your readers will dislike is almost as important as knowing what they do like: avoid picking fights with your readers. If you know you have a disagreement with one of your readers, can you leave that disagreement out of your work to focus on something that you both agree on?

Write to people who are interested

You may know exactly who is going to read your work, and hopefully they are supportive and encouraging (sadly, not all professors are). Regardless of your real audience, you can imagine that you are writing to ideal readers—readers who are interested and supportive, not readers who will attack your every premise and demand that you defend every statement. If you write about a specific topic, imagine writing to other people who have written on the topic, and to people who share some of your views—your heroes, the people whose work you model—rather than imagining writing to someone who will attack your choice of topic or theory.

It's always possible that you have a professor who is hostile to some idea, theory, or method you're using, and then it's necessary to write defensively. But even in such situations you want to minimize defensive writing. As much as possible, think about what you need to say to a knowledgeable and interested audience that is open to your ideas.

This exercise in imagining that you're writing to a supportive audience shapes what you would include in your draft (more discussion of what you do, less defense of your choices), and it also provides a much better emotional environment in which to work. If you write each sentence fearing a critic, you'll feel much different than if you write anticipating positive interest.

Conflicts

No-one writes for a singular audience, and sometimes a larger audience has its own internal variation—one reader wants one thing, one wants another. This is an additional complexity to be negotiated, but it's not usually an insurmountable issue. Try to keep a balance and keep an eye on the different needs of different members of your audience, and mostly keep an eye on your story: what do you want to tell?

Exercises (15–30 minutes)

Who are your different audiences? List different audiences for your work, starting with the individual professors who will read it (if you know). Then consider other people who might read it (any fellow students? working groups or seminar groups? administrators, including the IRB? conference organizers?). And finally list people who you would like to read your work (e.g., scholars you admire).

Are there any audiences that you would not want to write for? Do you have to write for any of those audiences? How does your writing change if you imagine writing to a hostile audience?

Focus on your own work

Writing for an audience—especially a hostile one—can distract from the core of what you are doing. If you're writing about your own research project, write about your own research project, not other people's work! This is not to say that you ignore suggestions and refuse to discuss the issues that interest others, but rather to say that those suggestions are all contextualized with respect to the project that you are working on and remain true to your vision.

You may be talking about other literature, but it is always with a selfish focus, in the sense that your work always makes its way into the conversation, and generally does so quickly.

If you're discussing the research question used by some author, do so with respect to your work: "The question and test posed by Turing, are a starting point for this research." "The results of AuthorA indicate a trend that this study will examine."

In this vein, I would suggest that one common problem for many dissertation writers is over-discussion of the methods and results of other studies. There are many times when a detailed discussion of someone else's methods or results is necessary. But those details can often distract from the focus on your own work: if an author makes a conclusion that is important to you, it may not be necessary to discuss all the details of that research. If it is the conclusion that is important to you, then discuss the conclusion. If you want to challenge some aspect of the method or the results, then certainly get as deep into the details as you want. But if what really matters to you is some conclusion that you accept, then details about method or results might not be important.

If, for example, you have a dozen sources that did an empirical study of pedagogical method, and they generally agree on its value in a certain context, and you want to translate that pedagogy to a slightly different context, it may be better not to detail all the results and methods of those twelve sources.

Yes, it might be relevant to write a long series of paragraphs that say:

> AuthorE and AuthorF used a qualitative method. The method involved ... Their results showed a wide range of different response of positive character...
>
> AuthorG and AuthorH in a quantitative longitudinal study, administered ... Their results showed ...
>
> AuthorI performed a quantitative study ...

Such a series of paragraphs can be deadly dull, can take several pages, and if the only real conclusion that you draw from them is, "Several different studies have shown positive results using this pedagogy," then do you really need that detail? Maybe you can just write: "Several different studies have shown positive results (AuthorE & Author F, 2000; AuthorG & AuthorH, 2005; AuthorI, 2010; etc.)."

Such a generalization does not stop you from singling out any study that has some specific details that strike you as particularly important. If there is some element of the methods or the results that specifically influenced some aspect of your work, of course you will discuss that in detail—but that's because then there is a specific focus on your own work: "The study by AuthorI particularly showed good results with students in the population that interests me."

Any discussion of any author should pretty quickly lead to some topic that you can say, "this is central to my work."

Exercises (5 minutes, repeat as useful)

Identify a source that you want to use. Write a sentence that explains how that work shapes your own research. What about the work is important to your own research? What about that work is tangential to your own research?

Paraphrasing

Many writers struggle to find the balance between quoting and paraphrasing. On the whole, my recommendation is to paraphrase if you can. If there is a quotation that is particularly memorable, then perhaps it's worth quoting, but on the whole, use your own words and your own voice. Paraphrasing is an expression of your own voice. Although a paraphrase is an attempt to express someone else's ideas, your choice of paraphrase involves your personal interpretation of the other person's words, and thus expresses your own voice. So, when possible, paraphrasing will help you focus on your own voice and on your own reasons for using the work you're paraphrasing.

Imagine talking with a colleague, fellow student, or professor about your ideas: you probably wouldn't use quotations—you would likely be focusing on your own ideas and interpretations. But if, in the course of such a discussion, you spontaneously recalled a specific quotation, then you would definitely want to think about using that specific quotation when you write, because it was embedded in your memory and was therefore having a strong influence.

Setting limits on the length of your discussion of literature helps avoid the worst dangers of over-quotation. If you're keeping your work tight and focused on your own reasoning, then you won't have space for too many long quotations.

I think people are in greatest danger of over-quotation if they are using too many sources (perhaps defensively). If you are trying to talk about every possible variation on an idea, then precise quotation is helpful in differentiating individual voices. This can often lead to a laundry-list approach to the discussion of literature, with a series of different scholars being discussed in turn, with quotations being used to help make clear differences that may not be crucial to your work. Such lists are boring to read, and usually only tangentially relevant to the work at hand. If you're quoting multiple scholars to help differentiate some fine distinction between them, then ask yourself if that fine distinction is crucial to your own research. Did that fine distinction have any direct impact on the specific questions you are asking? If so, then you may well want to quote. But if that fine distinction is only relevant to a more general discussion of variation in a large field of scholars, you might want to paraphrase, or even cut the discussion of that fine point entirely.

Exercises (1 minute, repeat as necessary)

Are there any ideas that you associate with a specific quotation? What's the quotation? These are ideas for which quotation will be excellent.

Are there ideas that you can paraphrase? Write a paraphrase of that idea. Is it a good paraphrase?

Look back at some of your old writing and look at where you used quotations. Could you have paraphrased?

Project 6: writing with literature

Who are your most important sources?

Pick the two to four most important sources that you use in your research.

For each work:

1. Give a basic summary.
2. Who is the main audience for the work? What other audiences might be interested? Is this work central in your research community, or is it something you're bringing in from outside?
3. Why is this work important to you?
4. What can you take from it that will help you develop your own research? Are you just taking main ideas or are you also taking ideas about how to structure your research project?

Notes

1 What profession doesn't require convincing people that the job is being done well? Of course, doing the job well is important, too, but it's pretty much impossible to escape the need to communicate about what you do, so developing your ability as a writer is a worthwhile investment of effort.
2 Having too much to say is a problem for many writers, not only in dealing with the literature but in trying to express their own ideas, too.
3 I believe that one of the main causes of writer's block is having too much to say, and one of the least common causes is having too little to say.
4 Unless, of course, your focal interest is that big debate. If your research is, for example, to give a conclusive argument for one side in a controversy, then you do want to get into details of that big debate. But don't argue big debates that you can avoid.
5 From John Page, "The East Asian Miracle: Four Lessons for Development Policy." In *NBER Macroeconomics Annual 1994*, Volume 9, Stanley Fischer and Julio J. Rotemberg, eds. (pp. 219–282). Cambridge, MA: MIT Press, p. 223.
6 Defining categories is tricky. A discussion of many theoretical issues related to defining categories can be found in George Lakoff's *Women, Fire, and Dangerous Things*.
7 As mentioned earlier, this phrase—"outside the scope of this work"—is an invaluable tool to the academic writer. Where can you use it?

Writing a literature review

The rest of the book has been generally concerned with processes—research, reading, writing—and the importance of practice. Now, in this final chapter, the focus shifts to a specific object: a written literature review, and how to write it. As to the second point—how to write a literature review—my partial answer, predictably, is "practice." But this chapter's discussion of the issues involved in writing a literature review offers more detailed suggestions for your efforts.

The crucial question for this chapter is, "what is a literature review?" The better your sense of what you're trying to create, the better your ability to act effectively as you move toward that goal. This book had its genesis in this question: it grew out of notes written to help a student writing a "literature review" chapter for her dissertation. Writing those notes forced me to think more closely about literature reviews, and about different types of literature review, especially which type of literature review was most appropriate for a dissertation. As I considered that question, I discovered numerous resources about writing literature reviews, many claiming to describe the literature review for a dissertation, but I found relatively few that matched my vision for a dissertation literature review (the APA publication manual's description of the "background" section of an article is one source that generally agrees with my view–albeit in a very brief discussion).

Herein lies a problem: different people have different ideas of what a literature review should be. Because there are a variety of published views of what goes into a dissertation literature review, I cannot make any suggestion without contradicting someone! Whether your literature review will get accepted depends on the person reviewing it, who may or may not agree with me. In this chapter, I am going to discuss different types of literature reviews, and will recommend a specific type of literature review that has an important role in scholarly literature. But what is important for you is to write the kind of literature review that will suit your purposes—and that means being sensitive to your context and community.

This chapter makes suggestions for writing a literature review that might be a good place to start your work on your literature review, even if your professors ask for something different than what I suggest. Throughout this chapter, I will emphasize keeping a tight focus and limiting the material you try to cover, so as a starting place for practice, my suggestions might help you get moving, and then if your professors want more or something different, you can expand from the briefer foundation.

Throughout this chapter, my primary focus will be on a specific type of literature review whose purpose is to explain the reasoning behind a specific research project (your dissertation), which I call a "research background literature review," and which is the appropriate kind of literature review to write if you are proposing or presenting a research project. There are other different types of literature reviews, and this chapter has little to say about them, beyond a basic description to differentiate them from the research background reviews. So, let's start this discussion by talking about different types of literature review.

What is a literature review?

Earlier, I discussed writing with purpose suitable to context. If you have to write a "literature review," it's crucial to know what is expected, why you are doing it, and what you hope to accomplish with it.

When looking at "literature reviews" as specific pieces of writing, the product depends on a variety of concerns. What is the purpose for the written work? Who is reading it? How much material does it cover? What goes in it? In extreme cases, the words "literature review" could reasonably be applied to a review of a single piece of writing, or to an annotated bibliography, but those are generally not what is expected of a "literature review."

As I see it, there are three basic classes of literature review in scholarly writing: Summary Overview, Research Background, and Research Study.

The first class—the summary or survey overview—surveys different ideas found in some body of literature on a given subject. It is not, generally speaking, primary, independent research. It reviews and summarizes what has been published by others on a subject without aspiring to provide any novel analytical insight. Summary overviews are common in textbooks, which often try to give a sense of the range of ideas in the literature. The summary overview is also often assigned as course work for students. It is

general and balanced, in the sense that it doesn't generally show preference
for one voice over another (though a survey can be critical in the sense of
identifying stronger vs. weaker research).

The second class—the research background review—is what
I recommend for the literature review in a doctoral dissertation. It provides background for a specific study by discussing the ideas that helped
define the research questions. Its purpose is to explain the intellectual
sources that inform a specific research project. It is the sort of literature
review that is used in standard five-chapter empirical study dissertations
(and in standard three-chapter dissertation proposals), as well as in most
empirical studies presented in APA journals (the *APA Publication
Manual* suggests that authors "Describe relevant scholarship").[1] This is
the kind of literature review that is the main focus of this chapter (and
this book, at least to the extent that this kind of literature review reflects
your research design decisions).

The final class—the research study—is the formal and methodical analysis
of a body of literature that is an empirical research study in its own right.
Such studies—meta-analyses and other related methods—use published literature as the data for systematic analyses. The purpose of such studies is to
develop new knowledge and to draw conclusions from newly gathered
empirical evidence. Research study reviews are generally considered original
research, and a research study review of sufficient scope can be a dissertation
project or work for publication. Such studies and their methods are outside
the scope of this book. The written versions of this kind of literature review
(from proposals to final drafts) will include a research background literature
review to help explain why the study was carried out.

In the rest of the chapter, I am going to focus on research background literature reviews. Research background reviews are the one type
of review that supports the development of a specific research project.
A summary review will just lead to a lot of reading without drawing
a conclusion. And a research study review, which is a type of empirical
study, requires a theoretical foundation derived from the community discourse, a foundation which is described by a research background review.

Exercises (10 minutes)

Which kind of literature review do you think you should be writing?
This book argues in favor of writing a research background review, but
the book also argues that you develop your own voice and vision. Does
your vision of a literature review agree or disagree with the suggestions

of this book? What issues seem important in determining what kind of literature review to write?

What is the purpose of your literature review? What is its context? Who is its audience? How does your planned review satisfy your audience?

The purpose of a research background literature review

The literature review supporting a research study—the second chapter of many doctoral dissertations—typically follows preliminary introductory material. In shorter pieces and works in the humanities, the literature review is integrated with the introduction as part of the background material describing your own research. The purpose of this sort of literature review, as already mentioned, is to use the literature to explain why your research project asks the questions it does.

As discussed, research is conducted within a community. It is shaped by ideas that shape the work of the research community and responds to questions asked in that community. Academic writing is often framed in impersonal terms, supporting the myth that "the facts speak for themselves." But facts don't speak or write. Authors do.

The choices you have made in designing your research—your choice of heroes to follow, of gaps in the literature to pursue, and of questions to explore—all have some relationship to the work that has come before you and inspired you. But they also grow out of your individual vision about which questions are important and the ideas that led to those choices.

The purpose of a research background literature review is to explain that reasoning and those choices to the reader through a comparison with other research, particularly the research that most strongly guided you. In a way, the purpose of a research background literature review is parallel to the purpose of a methods section: the literature review discusses the theoretical choices that shaped the project, and the methods section discusses the methodological choices that shaped the project.[2] Since the purposes of the two chapters are parallel, so is the scope and structure of the material covered. Think about the methods: do you discuss a complete history of all possible methods, or do you focus on the specific methodological choices that you made? The same perspective holds for a literature review: it's not a complete overview of debates in the field; it's a description of your specific project.

So, for example, if you are planning on assessing the quality of an intervention used in your field (e.g., a treatment program, an educational program, a plan for urban development, etc.), you will cite people who express concern with the same problem and who express desire for an intervention. You will cite people who have suggested interventions, and share their concerns on issues with interventions that led to your interest in a specific intervention. You will cite people who have talked about the specific intervention, and perhaps respond to questions they ask, or to some problem in their work. In the conversation expressed in the literature, which voices have impressed you as a model to emulate or a foil to contrast?

Or, for example, if you are planning on critical engagement with a given text, you might write about literature that discusses the text—maybe expressing a view that you would like to explore further; maybe expressing an idea that you want to alter or correct or contradict—or you might write about literature that suggests ideas that you want to apply to analysis of your chosen text. What you write is a conversation with the people whose writing influenced you. When you were reading, you were listening to the conversation. Now you're speaking, and you want to make it clear to whom you are responding: "Dr.X said that ..." and "Dr.Y proposed ...." The literature review chapter is the time to reflect the voices that you have heard. You reflect what you read, and share with the reader which of the ideas you accept, and which ideas lead you to the questions you want to ask in your own research.

Hopefully all these citations will naturally flow from your recognition of their influence on your work—if, for example, you are inspired by the work of Michel Foucault, then you would cite Foucault out of your sense that his ideas help you understand important issues. Citations should not be made just because you think, "I need to make some citations." If you have been developing a practice of examining how your ideas relate to other ideas expressed in the scholarly conversation, then this should not be too difficult.

Dissertation or thesis vs. publication

If one of your purposes is to get your work accepted, then you want to meet your audience's expectations. Professors reviewing student work have different interests, motivations, and corresponding expectations than do editors or peer reviewers. These differences stem from the varied purposes assumed for the publication: a dissertation or thesis is explicitly a test of student ability, where the "teachers" are explicitly defined as superior in qualification; while a journal article is supposedly the work of a qualified member of the community, which is why such journals are "peer reviewed." This difference in relationships can influence what is expected of your work.

With respect to the literature review, a professor reviewing a student and a dissertation might expect a general literature review to demonstrate the student's general command of the field. By contrast, an editor or peer reviewer considering a work for publication wants to identify a work's novelty, and therefore wants focus on the original argument, evidence, and conclusions, with the minimum literature review needed to give a sense of position in the larger conversation. Understanding the expectations and desires of the people who will review your work provides guidance as to your choices in how to present it.[3]

In a dissertation, the expectations of professors/reviewers vary widely. Most professors, I think, will desire a research background review, or at least will accept a research background review. A sizable number, however, think of the dissertation literature review as a summary overview, and will request that of students. The notion that the dissertation literature review is a survey literature review is, I feel, too common.[4]

Scholars seeking publication do not have to recap their entire field of literature constantly when explaining their own research.[5] And therefore, in my opinion, dissertation writers shouldn't be trying to do that either. Scholars should efficiently represent the philosophical and methodological starting points of their research. The *APA Publication Manual* (multiple editions), when discussing the "background" an author should give to explain a work, says that one should assume that the audience is knowledgeable (and therefore a general survey is unnecessary). This seems like an assumption that is efficient for both reader and writer: if we assume that the audience is knowledgeable, discussion can focus on salient issues more quickly, spending less time on giving general context.

If you are explicitly asked to write a summary overview review for your dissertation, as a matter of strategy, I suggest that you start by writing a research background review. If you write a good research background review that makes a good case for your research project, there's a decent chance it will be acceptable to your readers even if they had originally asked for a survey review. Sometimes, I think, professors (and others) aren't really clear on what makes a literature review work well, so they ask for a summary overview when they actually want a research background review (or at least will accept a research background review). Worst comes to worst, if you write a research background review explaining your own project, and your professor wants more of a survey overview or wants you to add some specific piece of literature, you can do so.[6] In such a case, the time you spent writing a research background review is still well-spent for its role in helping you design your project, and will serve well if you need to submit a proposal to an IRB before doing empirical research with subjects, or if you are applying for funding—even if your professor wants a survey overview, other important people are going to want a research background review.

Exercises (15 minutes)

Have you received any outside guidance about literature reviews (university or department guidelines, publications about literature reviews)? What do those sources suggest? Do you agree with those sources? Why or why not? If those sources are your professors, how will you try to satisfy their expectations?

Writing about search terms

In the previous section, I said that some professors may not clearly understand what they're asking for when they ask for a literature review, and they ask for something more like a survey review than a research background review. That understates the issue a bit, I think: a lot of guidance on literature reviews doesn't clearly differentiate between different kinds of literature review, and the suggestion that the dissertation literature review is a sort of survey review is pretty common in books and advice found on university websites.[7] As a result of this view, it is becoming more common for professors to ask the writer of a dissertation literature review to provide search terms that were used to determine inclusion in the literature review, and I think this is problematic for writers who are doing a research background literature review.

For "Summary Overview" and "Research Study" literature reviews, it is appropriate and sometimes very important to explain search terms along with all methods and inclusion/exclusion criteria used in gathering the literature analyzed in the study.[8] Such projects are generally guided by a formal method, necessitating formally defined criteria for inclusion/exclusion of material. And when you are following a specific, formal process, it is important to describe that process, including discussion of the methods of selecting literature.[9]

But research design is not a formal process, and so research background literature reviews, which are supposed to explain the decisions that shaped a specific research project, are not describing the results of a systematic process, but rather the distillation of a years-long process of learning that started even before you entered a graduate program. The sources that inform your own research project did not come from a specific structured search or set of searches, they came from your life as a student and scholar.

You might be able to work backward from the sources you use to a set of searches that would produce those results, but that's not the point of discussing search terms.

The most important sources that influence your choice of a project usually precede the definition of a project—they are the sources that led you into your program of study and to your choice of topic. They are choices made over years and they come out of theoretical foundations that are crucial to any specific project. Your definition of the terms and constructs you study, and your choices of material/data for examination and modes of examination are all products of your years of interaction with your research community. These are the ideas that led you to define a project, and therefore they are the ideas that belong in a research background review. But they are not ideas that you found through some single specific search for material to read.

It should be obvious that I think that search terms have no good place in a research background literature review. If a professor tells you that your literature review needs to discuss search terms, that can be a problem. It's probably worth trying to explain to them how the material that you're including is the material that has influenced you over time, not just material found in a specific search. This might be most effective with respect to discussing theoretical constructs because you can say something like: "Well, I have to discuss inquiry-based pedagogy, but that's something I learned before I started this project." And once you convince them of that first step, it might be easier to get them to give up the need for search terms.

Sometimes professors who aren't entirely clear on what they want in a literature review will ask for a summary overview and for search terms, but they will accept a well-constructed research background review. If a research background review does a good job of explaining why a study should be carried out, the reader may be sufficiently persuaded to accept the project, even if the literature review is not what the professor had requested. The more persuasive your explanations of why you did what you did, the less likely it is you will receive complaints.[10]

Exercises (10 minutes)

Do you need to write about search terms? Why or why not? What aspects of your process in gathering literature were pre-planned? Were any parts of your literature review process shaped by discoveries that you did not anticipate when you started?

Voice

This section is concerned with what is largely a matter of presentation—a rhetorical concern. How do you write about other literature when you're trying to describe your project?

Throughout this book, I emphasize the need for you to focus your attention on your own project and how the literature you read relates to your project and your reasoning more generally. But in a "literature review" you can focus on yourself too much. Even though the purpose of the literature review is to explain your own reasoning and your own project, the discussion in it is framed in terms of other people's work.

The discussion focuses on specific pieces of the literature and relates them to your study; for example, "Dr.X defines the major construct of this study in the following manner: ... Although other definitions have been proposed, full discussion of that debate is outside the scope of this work." Or, "We briefly discuss the variety of different definitions of our main construct, and then focus on that of Dr.X, which is used in this study."

Comparison between introduction and literature review

The first two chapters of a standard empirical study dissertation—the introduction and literature review—share something of their purpose: they both try to draw your reader in by explaining your research. Both the introduction and literature review explain your motivation and reasoning for doing the work. But they go about that task differently. In the introduction, the focus is on the main ideas: what is the research question, why is it formed that way, and why do you care? You want to deliver those points as clearly and as straightforwardly as possible. When you get to the literature review, having already stated your main points, you now have the task of presenting those same points through the lens of the literature. If you said in the introduction: "I am doing this study because questionX has not been answered in the literature, and because there is value in answering questionX for reasons A, B, and C," then in the literature review you're going to come at the same point, but (as much as possible) you'll bring in your sources more directly. For example:

> AuthorA suggests that questionX$_1$ is important, when she writes "questionX$_1$ is important" (year, p.#). And AuthorB suggests that questionX$_2$ is important when he writes "question X$_2$ is important" (year, p.#). While there are good reasons to keep questionX$_1$ and questionX$_2$ separate (see, for example, AuthorA, year, p.#; AuthorB, year, p.#; AuthorC, year), it has been suggested that questionX$_3$, which conflates the two, also is of interest (AuthorD, year).

The basic content is similar. The framing and level of detail are different.

> **Exercises** (10 minutes; repeat)
>
> Pick an idea or theory that you want to use that you can directly relate to a specific author. Write a sentence about that idea/theory that would be suitable for an abstract or introduction (a description of your work and where the idea/theory fits in your work). Write a sentence about that idea/theory that would be suitable for a research background literature review (a discussion of other people's ideas and how those other ideas relate to and influence your work).

How short can a literature review be?

In the previous chapter, I suggested the importance of target lengths and of writing short drafts. I'm going to re-emphasize that here, but I'm going to place a greater emphasis on writing a short literature review—as short as possible, not just the early drafts but the final one. You want to focus as precisely as possible on the foundations of your research project and thus keep your literature review as small as possibly appropriate. But what is appropriate?

Context determines what is appropriate. I have already argued that you don't want to give too much material to your readers, and that you want to try to give them what they expect. What is expected is very much a matter of the specific readers and the immediate community to which you belong. If you're writing your dissertation or thesis, that means understanding the expectations for dissertations in your department.

A quick review of other similar works can be valuable for assessing expectations. If you're writing a dissertation, look at other dissertations written by recent graduates of your department. How long are their literature reviews? If, instead, you're writing a journal article, you can look at articles in that journal to see how much space has been used for previous literature reviews/background. How long is the longest? The median? The shortest?

What you see by reviewing these documents that exemplify the work published in the same venue that you want to publish, is the practical manifestation of the expectations of the reviewers. If you find that the longest literature review in recent dissertations in your department is forty pages, that indicates that you may not benefit from writing more. If the shortest is five pages, then you can be pretty certain that your audience may complain about less. That being said, I always suggest writing the shortest work that you can, so if you could write a literature review shorter than five pages, and it felt intellectually solid, to you, I would suggest submitting it just to see what happens. Adding material to a draft is almost always easier than cutting it. Could you get away with writing a literature review as short as the shortest from previous dissertations? Could you write a first draft of about 75% of the length of the shortest? Set a good, short target length for your literature review.

Short drafts also have the advantage of being less likely to bore your reader, offering less chance that you will say something problematic, and reducing the time needed for writing about the works of others—time that could be spent writing about your own work and developing your project. For all these reasons, I strongly recommend setting target lengths for the literature review that seem too short.

> **Exercises** (Due to possible difficulties in finding appropriate dissertations, step 1 might take some time; 10 minutes for steps 2 through 5).
>
> Step 1: Look at about five dissertations recently filed in your department, preferably some that were chaired by your dissertation chair. How long are their literature reviews?
>
> Step 2: Set a target length for your completed final literature review.
>
> Step 3: Write a quick outline/bullet list of the main points/main sections of your literature review.
>
> Step 4: Set a target length for the first draft of your literature review.
>
> Step 5: How long should the first draft of each section of the literature review be?

Start from the core, and work outward

As I've suggested, in my experience, people often struggle with their literature review because they try to do too much, not too little. And, although I've known people who were asked to add material to their literature review, I don't know (or at least remember) anyone who had significant problems because their literature review was too short. I have already argued for the importance of minimal drafts, so this may all be redundant; a danger I'll risk to approach the same issue from a slightly different angle.

Start with a direct model

Try starting by focusing on one or a few pieces of literature that specifically ask for a research project like the one you're doing. Because a research background literature review is not about general discussion, focus on the specific piece or pieces of published research that most explicitly and obviously relate to the kind of research you are doing.

Are there any studies that match almost all your concerns? An original study could be generated by starting from a single model work that you read, copying all the research design factors, and adding a new one of interest. And, if you have been finding direct models in the literature, then, when writing a literature review, you want to structure it around and focus it on those direct models. You can structure your review to cover the same general sources and ideas that they did, with the addition of any concerns that you might add to those of the research you're using. If your main sources are "talking to" (citing) sources, it makes sense for your work to try to "talk" to the same sources. This allows you to better fit into a coherent conversation.

Start with your foundations

If you can't pick one single source as a model, another way to structure a research background literature review is to focus on the works that are foundational. Maybe you have a few sources that you're mixing together in some way. Or a main theory that is central to your work. These specific foundational works can provide a focus for a literature review that describes the reasoning behind your research project.

Any discussion you add beyond these foundations should be driven by a sense of necessity—a sense that your work won't make sense unless you add it.

A research background literature review is building a conceptual foundation for your project, so what are the specific sources on which you rely? Building a foundation from specific sources can help you avoid getting sucked into other people's debates.

Don't start with general themes

Many writers try to be organized and systematic by defining a set of necessary themes/issues in their work, and then try to give a general literature review for each theme. For example a psychologist interested in using a specific intervention for a specific population, might try to generally review issues related to the intervention and then generally review issues related to the specific population. Such a strategy loses focus on your specific work and invites a discussion of many works that are not crucial to your own project.

While it can be useful to speak of whole groups of scholars or entire categories of other sorts—genres, for example—such discussion can also draw you into discussion of internal debates and debates over terminology. If you try to engage with a whole class or category, it's easy to start to consider where to draw boundaries or what characteristics define them, but those questions take you away from the central concerns of your work, and can take a lot of time discussing peripheral fine distinctions.

Focus on the individual and the specific pieces of research that are most important to you! Start from the central works, and extend outward from there. Trying to define the boundaries or characteristics of a class or category can be extremely difficult. Trying to give an overview of a whole range of ideas can be time consuming. Trying to define boundary conditions or specific characteristics can lead to debate. If you focus on specific exemplars it is much easier to keep the discussion focused. Using an exemplar allows you to focus on a more limited set of material, and on the issues that are of greatest importance to you.

I think this point is of particular value for people in the humanities, who often get into genre debates. Genre debates do not easily resolve and they often become emotionally charged. And perhaps worst of all, they are rarely the issue of real interest. Sometimes the genre debate really is the issue of importance, but in my experience, people who struggle with genre debates are actually interested in specific works, not all members of the genre.

Exercises (5 minutes; repeat as appropriate)

Pick one specific reading from your reading list, preferably one that you would like to use. What are some of the questions that it raises for you? What are some research projects that those questions suggest? If you have already defined your own project, in what way does that one specific source shape your own work?

Writing a literature review—structural concerns

The precise structure of a literature review is dependent on context and subject, so I don't think that there is any general template to follow. Nonetheless, I'm going to lay out some very general principles for planning the structure for a research background literature review in a doctoral dissertation. Because of variations in research, the structure of a literature review can only be described in the most general terms. Rather than offering a template, I want to discuss some structural issues.

Length

One thing we can assess fairly well is the length of a literature review. As I have already suggested, the best plan of action is to get your target lengths by looking at works in your specific community. Find out how long literature reviews are in your program and use that for guidance.

Here I am going to make very general statements based on general estimates, that may, nonetheless, be useful. Doctoral dissertations vary in length across fields, but it would be reasonable to say that a practical maximum is in the range of 80,000 words.[11] In the U.K., universities commonly place an absolute limit, often of 80,000 words (e.g., Cambridge University). Similar limits are stated at universities in Canada (e.g., University of British Columbia). These are maximum limits, which implies that shorter works are acceptable. To my knowledge, U.S. universities don't generally set similar limits.

If your whole dissertation is going to be 80,000 words, and you imagine the literature review as taking 10%–20% of the whole, that would be 8,000 to 16,000 words for the literature review. There may be cases where the literature review might take a greater portion of the whole than 20%, but remember that the dissertation is to present your own work, not to review other people's.

But if the maximum expected/accepted is 80,000 words, why set out planning to write all 80,000 words? If 80k is the maximum, why not aim to make your final draft somewhat shorter—70,000 words, for example? That would put the literature review at 7,000 to 14,000 words. And then taking into account my earlier suggestion to set the target for early drafts at a fraction of the final, you might decide that your first complete draft of the dissertation will be about two-thirds that length, or in the range of 45,000 words, with perhaps 4,500 to 9,000 words in the first draft of literature review. If the range is from 4,500 to 9,000 words, you can aim at 4,500, or about 15 pages using double-spaced lines and a 12-point font.

General areas of content

There are several different areas that a research background literature review must cover. Firstly, there is need for the general theoretical foundations— the major theories that shape the approach. Then there is the need to get into the specific details of interest and any variables or constructs that will be central to the work.

Discussions of major theoretical foundations should be kept brief. They should discuss the big ideas that frame the work as a whole.[12] In many studies there are a few different theoretical frameworks that come into play. A study of some classroom intervention would probably rely on a theory of pedagogy and on a theory of human development.[13] A study of archaeo-logical history might combine some theory of social forces with some theory of environmental change. Every large set of theories you use deserves at least a few sentences to discuss some of the voices in the literature. Give a solid description of how these theories shape your research so your reader understands the basic ideas of what you're doing. Do not give extensive dis-cussion of debates on these large theories and don't get sucked into details. Explain your foundations, don't debate them.

I would say that major theories should be capped at about 25% of the total length of your literature review.

Once you've set the stage with a brief overview of the main theoretical principles, then you can move on to the details of your specific study. And there will be lots of different specifics. Every single choice you made that focused and limited your choice of study might be worthy of discussion. If you are interested in some intervention (whether pedagogical, clinical, or other), that intervention probably has several characteristics that are worthy of discussion. If you are planning on using that intervention with a specific population, the characteristics of that population are all worthy of discus-sion. And then, if you are interested in specific dynamics, you have to direct attention to those specific dynamics (how do the people interact with the intervention? What are the issues you are looking for in that interaction?).

The discussion of the different specific characteristics is important. And there are typically going to be a pretty large number of characteristics that matter, so get to the main points of each characteristic. If there is some spe-cific characteristic or variable of particular interest to your work, then it's worth a discussion of theoretical debates on that specific variable, but other-wise, it's important to give the reader an overview of all the general charac-teristics, without burying them in details of work that you don't use.

In short, the literature review starts with brief discussion of large theories, and then is fleshed out with coverage of the various specific details that define the project.

General narrative structure

One general statement can be made about the structure of a literature review: start with the big ideas that give a framework for all the rest. Beyond that, there is no strict rule for how to order the contents of the literature review: there is rarely a clear right answer for the question of which variable to discuss first. One of the difficulties of writing (not just literature reviews), is that ideas are typically intertwined and interdependent, but to write them out, you're forced to organize them in a linear fashion. Because of the interdependence, it's hard to know which idea should be discussed first. Almost any outline that you choose will have some strengths and some weaknesses, so don't look for a perfect outline, just make one and try to stick to it.[14]

Although the outline of a literature review can't easily be generalized, there are some narrative basics to remember. Any literature review (and many other large segments of writing) can use the basic introduction-body-conclusion structure for the work as a whole, and an introduction can have a basic two-part structure:

1. General discussion of main point to set context.
2. Overview of different aspects of the main point to be covered.

This opening can be followed by a series of sections, each focused on one of the different areas of interest. You can budget perhaps 10%–20% of the length of any given section to its introduction.[15] If you have planned for a section to take 1,000 words, then you'll have about 800 words to go into detail if you have an overview of this sort. You don't want to overdo the introductions, but it's valuable to give your readers a sense of context for the works you discuss.

Each subsection can open with a very similar structure:

1. Discussion of the specific aspect of the project in the context of the larger project.
2. Overview of different areas of the specific aspect to be covered.

This is, of course, essentially a repeat of the larger structure—it is a formula that works for subsections, too, if they're long enough. It's a formula that dedicates a good deal of attention to what might be called the "connective tissue" of the writing: writing that explains how each little part connects to the other parts. But it also helps anchor what you discuss in the specifics of your study: by opening each subsection with a brief statement of how this particular subset of literature relates to your project, you're less likely to go too far off on digressions.

Structure the literature review around the ideas in your research question, and then bring in literature to suit that discussion.

Exercises (15 minutes)

Write a two-level outline for a research background literature review.

Define the target length.

List the main sections of the chapter (first level).

Set target lengths for each section.

For each main section, list subsections (when appropriate; second level).

Set target lengths for each subsection.

Write an introductory sentence that explains your purposes for the literature review.

Project 7: writing a skeleton literature review

Task: Write a short, skeletal literature review for a research project.
Suggested length: 1,500 words.

Guiding suggestions
Hopefully you are already working on your own research design, and so you can use your current research project as a basis for this short review. If you are not already working to define your own research project, well, there's no time like the present to start trying, and you're not committed simply on the basis of this short review project.

- What is the project? And what is the research question?
- What are the main general theories that set the context for your work?
- What are the main specific characteristics/dimensions of your study (i.e., any specific variables, any specific characteristics of your data)?
- Write an outline. What are the main sections?
- For each section and subsection write an introductory sentence or paragraph that explains how that section/subsection helps define your specific research project. Make a prioritized list of the three to five most important sources for that section.

Notes

1 *Publication Manual of the American Psychological Association* (6th edition). Washington, DC: APA, 2010. p.28: "Discuss the relevant related literature, but do not feel compelled to include an exhaustive historical account." The very presence of that line suggests that many writers did include exhaustive historical accounts in their work.

2 This is an imperfect parallel. Operationalization, the crucial translation of an intellectual construct into an operational variable in an empirical study, is a bridging of these two domains.

3 Guidance, but not commands! You don't have to meet people's expectations. It's best, however, to violate expectations by choice rather than by accident.

4 As I've mentioned earlier, the dissertation project, and independent research generally, ought not to be about proving the author's credentials, it ought to be about the research project.

5 Of course, if they're writing a textbook, that's a different story. If you wanted to write a textbook for a project, the textbook itself would include summary overview material. But the textbook proposal for a publisher would be a specific argument for the purpose of the book, with a review of similar textbooks and why yours is different/better. This material that you would use in a proposal for a publisher is a close parallel to a research background review, not a summary overview.

6 This strategy is more effective if, as suggested in the previous chapter, you write drafts quickly and submit them for feedback.

7 I hope you know that I disagree, but this book is more about learning to deal with a variety of situations as part of your practice. I think that writing a research background review will help because it focuses your efforts on designing your own project. Part of the practice of research is being able to judge when you can give your audience what you think they should get, and when you have to give them what they have asked for.

8 For a research study, inclusion criteria are pretty much essential, while for a summary overview, especially an informal one, such criteria might not be needed.

9 And it should be noted that in trying to write up such projects, you would have to write an explanation of why you chose the method and criteria that you used. That explanation would be a research background literature review.

10 Justice Potter's "I know it when I see it" principle can be taken from a slightly different angle: it can be about how it's hard to put something into words, even if we can identify it with confidence. From this perspective, some professors may know the right kind of literature review when they see it, but not be able to describe it.

11 Word counts are good for judging the length of a work because they are constant despite formatting manipulations. A lot of people like to write single spaced—you can put a lot more on a screen that way—but documents are expected to be double spaced. If you like to write single spaced, then using page counts for length means that you have to mess around with formatting to see how long the document is. Traditionally, a "page" is assumed to be 250 words, but in practice, double spaced, 12-pt font pages have in the range of 280 to 330 words, depending on the font.

12 Without getting dragged into any lengthy debate about the value of that big idea.
13 Such theories can be intertwined—Jean Piaget's theory of development was intertwined with his concerns for education—but they need not be.
14 There are times when it seems like a new and different outline will solve the problems faced in developing an outline into a piece of writing. The temptation to switch to a new outline should be indulged with caution: the new outline is likely to have its own problems that you will only see once you get deeply into it. You're better able to see the problems of the thing you're working on right now than you are able to anticipate the problems of a project you haven't yet started.
15 This is somewhat dependent on the size of the piece of writing. If your piece of writing is to be 100 words, or even 1,000, then 20% on the introductory sentences is totally reasonable. If your writing is going to be 10,000 words, then a 2,000-word introduction (20%) might be too long.

Conclusion

If I could give you a simple step-by-step method for doing research design or a literature review, I would. Methods are extremely powerful and useful, and if you can use them, it is highly recommended. But, as I have argued, methods cannot guide you through many of the difficult and crucial parts of research design and research practice. Because you can't rely on methods all the time, I have advocated treating research as a practice that helps you develop your skills and abilities so that you can work more effectively—both so that you can keep moving in places where methods don't serve, and you can work more easily on the myriad reading and writing tasks that every researcher faces.

At risk of redundancy, I will conclude by briefly restating my main points: 1) Practice; 2) Develop and clarify your own voice and vision; 3) Make your place in your community; 4) Finish projects.

1. **Practice:** Experiment, explore, and develop your own abilities and skills. A doctoral dissertation is, in part, intended for students to develop experience as an independent researcher. Focus on developing your skills and developing your own project.
2. **Develop your voice:** To do your own research, you need to follow your own vision. You will build a lot of that vision through understanding gained from others, but you have to trust and develop your own vision and your own voice, because those are necessary to guide you to original research. Practice explaining your ideas to others, and try to use literature in that process.
3. **Make your place in your community:** For all that you are an independent researcher, your research occurs in a community. Whether your audience at a given moment is one specific person, or a wider audience within your community, you benefit from having the skill to explain

what you are doing and why that exploration serves the community. This is, perhaps, most easily done by showing that other people in the community care about the same issues (by citing the literature). Being able to speak and write effectively about other people in your community is an invaluable skill, whatever your plans for your future career. Indeed, if you envision a professional career, skills as a reader of and writer about literature are valuable, even if you are never going to do another independent research project. In addition, you need the courage to put your original ideas out on public display. This takes confidence—a confidence that develops with practice.

4. **Finish projects:** To put your work on display for review—by submitting it to professors, to administrators, to journals, etc.—is to risk rejection and criticism. Nonetheless, it's to your benefit to take that risk. Developing a practice insulates you from anxiety surrounding a single project or task, because you know that you have, or will develop, the skills you need for that task. And understanding the limits on research and on research methods will help you make the practical decisions and compromises that must be made to bring a project to completion.

Suggested readings

Boice, Robert. (1990). *Professors as Writers*. Based on empirical observation and study of professorial writing, Boice's book details which practices lead to productive writing. If you're struggling with your writing, this is an excellent resource.

Feyerabend, Paul. (1975). *Against Method*. Feyerabend was a student of Karl Popper (see below). He rejected Popper's work on the grounds that scientists often violate the norms of their research community to advance their work, and argued for what he called "epistemological anarchy." His discussion of places where science steps aside from method was one of my primary influences in developing a focus on practice rather than method.

Foucault, Michel. (1970). *The Order of Things: An Archaeology of the Human Sciences*. Originally published in French in 1966 as *Les Mots et Les Choses* ("Words and Things"), Foucault's work looks at social and political forces that shaped development of "sciences," and what gets considered knowledge. Foucault proposes an *episteme*—a set of principles by which knowledge is judged—and how different *epistemes* change and are shaped by social, political, and historical factors.

Graff, Gerald, and Birkenstein, Cathy. (2006). *They Say/I Say*. This best-selling college-writing book is now in its fourth edition, so you may have seen it. It's light on theory and heavy on examples. The examples can be a little simplistic, but the general principles are excellent. If you're struggling with writing about literature and your research, its templates can help you focus on the conversational dimension of academic writing.

Kuhn, Thomas. (1962). *The Structure of Scientific Revolutions.* Kuhn's work was a history of science that introduced the notion of "scientific paradigms"—systems of scientific thought that maintain internal consistency—which periodically get overturned in "revolutions" in which new paradigms are adopted. According to Kuhn, paradigms cannot be measured against each other because each answers some questions that the other fails to answer. Most science, according to Kuhn, goes on within established communities that accept a single paradigm and judge research according to its relevance within that specific paradigm.

Lakoff, George. (1987). *Women, Fire, and Dangerous Things.* Lakoff's book discusses category structure through the lens of his work in cognitive linguistics. The early part of the book discusses different theories of categorization and difficulties with these theories. It looks at how words acquire meaning and thus can help make clear why definition of terms is so difficult.

Latour, Bruno. (1987). *Science in Action.* Latour discusses the crucial role of social and institutional forces in shaping the practice of science and what gets accepted as science.

Popper, Karl. (1959). *The Logic of Scientific Discovery.* Originally published in German in 1934, this is Popper's seminal work in philosophy of science, in which he lays out his principle of knowledge through falsification. Popper, who was knighted by Queen Elizabeth II, is regarded as one of the foremost 20th-century philosophers of science. His principle of falsification aspires to objectivity, but it relies upon a community of researchers to test hypotheses and to decide which hypotheses have been best tested.

Index

abstracts 62, 84, 86–88
ad hominem argument 35, 85; *see also* rhetoric
audience 32, 34, 54, 97, 98–99, 100, 115, 121, 124, 129, 130–133, 142

bibliographic software 72–73
bibliographies 89–90

certainty (logical/rational) 3, 5, 8–12, 14, 22, 31, 36, 42, 45, 56
citation 52; need for 63; rules governing 85; use of 100–101, 141
commitment 10, 28, 31–32, 49, 59, 71
common knowledge 63
community 3, 5, 10, 11–15, 45, 80–82; communicating with 42, 57, 62, 97, 103, 112; *see also* rhetoric; contribution to 28; finding place in 50, 156–157; *see also* confidence; influence of 6, 30, 139; *see also* professors; and literature 55, 86; standards of 8–9, 20, 47, 63, 79, 138, 141–142, 146, 150; writing about 53, 124, 127, 140–141
complexity 47, 56–57
conceptual framework *see* theoretical foundations
confidence 20, 36–37, 42, 45–46, 64, 78, 112
cooking 18–19, 28, 33, 115
copying *see* research models *and* rhetorical models

deadlines *see* schedule
decision making 20, 22, 23, 48, 49, 54, 68
deep reading 51, 82–84, 89, 94–110

definition (of terms, concepts) 57, 88, 100, 107, 144; committing to 49; and community 15; difficulty with 104–106; and generalization 128–129; sources for 101–102; variations in 10, 14, 46, 58–59, 124; *see also* operationalization
design, design theory 54, 58–59
discourse *see* community
dissertation 3, 19, 22, 37, 50, 128, 146; literature review for 139, 149–150
dissertation/thesis vs. publication 141–142
draft length 121–122, 146, 147, 150
drafts 19, 32, 117, 119
driving 47–48, 68, 95

emotion 32, 45, 52, 55, 77, 97, 125
empirical research 11–13, 15, 20, 105, 139, 145
evidence 8, 11–12, 15, 18, 34, 105, 107, 139
experimentation 12, 18, 37
exploratory reading 21, 29, 46, 48–49, 71
exploratory writing 117

facts 2, 3, 7–9, 140
falsification 12
feedback 112, 117, 119–120
fiction 2, 3, 7–9, 52
field of study 80–82
finding your own voice *see* personal voice

gaps in the literature 5, 10, 45, 50, 97, 140
generalization 12, 126, 127–128
grammar 21, 32, 33, 35, 118

Hume, David 12, 14, 52, 53, 97
humility 36

induction 11–12
instrumental reading 48–49; *see also*
    research models
interpretation 8, 46–47, 105; and
    commitment to 45; and paraphrasing
    134–135

jargon 57–58

Kant, Immanuel 12, 14, 52, 97, 98

learning 27–29, 52, 63, 69; in practice
    18, 20
legal writing 56
life decisions 22, 37; *see also* skill,
    development of *and* topic, choice of
limitations (of research) 8, 9, 56–57
limits: of knowledge 6; philosophical 6,
    12, 36, 54; *see also* certainty (logical/
    rational); practical 22, 37, 51, 76,
    78–80, 96; *see also* resources; setting of
    69, 71, 124–126, 135; *see also* draft
    length *and* rhetorical models
literature review: process vs. product 70;
    as process 70; in research design 72;
    types of 137–139; length of 121–122,
    124, 135, 146–147, 150
literature search *see* search results *and*
    search terms
Logic of Scientific Discovery, The 9; *see also*
    Popper, Karl

managing resources *see* resources, use of
mixed methods 27
modeling research *see* research models
motivation 20–21, 34–35; in the
    literature 60, 87, 97–100, 107; writing
    about 131–132, 145

Newton, Isaac 4, 15, 30, 52

objective knowledge 10, 11–12
objectivity 3, 52, 55, 105, 131
operationalization 87, 88, 104–106; *see
    also* questions
originality in research 6, 15, 36, 49, 61;
    expectation for 50; and use of models
    95–96, 148
outlines 117, 151–152

paraphrasing 134–135
peer review 8, 57, 101, 104, 130–131,
    141–142
personal voice 23, 25, 33, 112, 116, 120,
    156–157; development of 42, 47;
    expression of 131; and paraphrasing
    134–135; *see also* confidence ; *and* ori-
    ginality in research
persuasion *see* rhetoric
Popper, Karl 9, 10, 12, 14, 52, 53
practice 11, 18–40, 47–48, 115,
    117–120, 156
professionals 19, 23, 78, 157
professors: and choice of topic 24;
    communication with 19, 120;
    expectations of 13, 52, 63–64, 79,
    101, 121, 128, 141–144; learning
    from 5, 6, 30, 62, 76; and research
    community 34; 112 ; *see also* audience
Protzen, Jean-Pierre 54
publication 34, 50, 139, 141–143
publication data 73, 84–86
purpose: awareness of 6; as a reader
    46–49; as a researcher 4, 19–21, 48,
    97; of research community 14; as
    a writer 32, 116–118, 138, 140–141

questions 5, 14; choice of 8, 15; *see also*
    topic, choice of; in the literature 13,
    24, 25, 49, 71, 133; multiplicity of 6,
    10, 21, 37, 51,71; for research 24,
    26–27, 104–106; *see also* operationali-
    zation; writing about *see* research
    background literature review
quotation *see* paraphrasing

record keeping 72–73
relevance, standards of 69, 74, 83
replication studies 95, 96
research background literature review:
    content of 150–151; definition of
    138–139; focus of 147–149; length of
    146–147, 150; purpose of 140–143;
    and search terms 143–144; structure of
    149, 151–152; writer's voice in
    145–146
research community *see* community
research methods 107–108, 143, 156,
    157; and audience 99; choice of 24,
    26–27, 49, 98; limits of 3, 20, 28; in
    the literature 25, 47, 88, 96; in
    reviewing literature 71; role of 7, 8, 18;

skill in use of 19, 28; writing about 117–118, 133–134, 140; *see also* research models
research models 49, 95–96
research question *see* questions
research study literature review 138–139, 143
resources: allocation of 22–23, 42, 51, 79; use of 18, 27, 29–30, 74, 83
rhetoric 34–36, 60, 124–126, 145
rhetorical models 96, 102–104
Rittel, Horst 54

schedules 38, 77, 120
search results 75, 76, 83, 84, 86
search terms 143–144
significance of studies *see* motivation
Simon, Herbert 54
skill, development of 18–21, 23, 28, 32–33
skimming 51, 89; vs. deep reading 82–84
speech vs. writing 32–33, 118–119
style 96, 99, 102–104
suggestions for future research *see* certainty (logical/rational)

summary overview literature review 138–139, 142–143
systematic literature review 71; *see also* research study literature review; *and* summary overview literature review

Tao Te Ching 9
telephone conversation 69, 101
theoretical foundations 6, 24, 42, 53–54, 100, 122–124, 144, 150–151
theoretical framework *see* theoretical foundations
thinking, writing and 31–32
topic, choice of 24, 98, 144; *see also* questions
trade-offs 24
Turing, Alan 105–106

uncertainty *see* certainty (logical/rational) *and* confidence

writer's block 112, 121
writing drafts 33, 63, 117–120, 121, 146–147, 150
writing quality 55–58, 63, 102, 119